Pakistani Folklore, including: Heer Ranjha, Mirza Sahiba, Sohni Mahiwal, Punjabi Kisse, Sucha Singh Soorma, Sanwal Sajal, Punjabi Folklore, Sassi Punnun, Dhaj, Ror Kumar, Shahrukh Husain, Jinn, One Thousand And One Nights, Hamzanama, Lake Saiful Muluk

Hephaestus Books

Contents

Articles

Heer Ranjha **1**

Heer Ranjha 1

Mirza Sahiba **4**

Mirza Sahiba 4

Sohni Mahiwal **6**

Sohni Mahiwal 6

Punjabi Kisse **9**

Punjabi Kisse 9

Sucha Singh Soorma **12**

Sucha Singh Soorma 12

Sanwal Sajal **16**

Sanwal Sajal 16

Punjabi folklore **17**

Punjabi folklore 17

Sassi Punnun **18**

Sassi Punnun 18

Dhaj, Ror Kumar **21**

Dhaj, Ror Kumar 21

Shahrukh Husain **23**

Shahrukh Husain 23

Jinn **24**

Jinn 24

One Thousand and One Nights **30**

One Thousand and One Nights 30

Hamzanama **53**

Hamzanama 53

Lake Saiful Muluk **55**

Lake Saiful Muluk 55

Churel **57**

Churel 57

Pakistani folklore **58**

Pakistani folklore 58

Ayyār **62**

Ayyār 62

Adam Khan and Durkhanai **64**

Adam Khan and Durkhanai 64

Yusuf Khan and Sherbano **65**

Yusuf Khan and Sherbano 65

Prince Saiful Malook and Badri Jamala **67**

Prince Saiful Malook and Badri Jamala 67

Noori Jam Tamachi **69**

Noori Jam Tamachi 69

The Tale of the Four Dervishes **70**

The Tale of the Four Dervishes 70

Yusuf and Zulaikha **72**

Yusuf and Zulaikha 72

Momal Rano **73**

Momal Rano 73

Umar Marvi **74**

Umar Marvi 74

LiLa Chanesar **76**

LiLa Chanesar 76

Hani and Sheh Mureed **78**

Hani and Sheh Mureed 78

References

Article Sources and Contributors 83

Image Sources, Licenses and Contributors 84

Heer Ranjha

Heer Ranjha

For 1970 Hindi movie of same name and characters, see Heer Raanjha.

Tilla Jogian, where Ranjha came

Example

The invocation at the beginning
(The Legends of the Panjab by RC Temple, Rupa and Company, Volume two, page 606)
Rag Hir Ranjha

> "Awal-akhir naam Allah da lena, duja dos Muhammad Miran Tija naun mat pita da lena, unha da chunga dudh sariran
> Chautha naun an pani da lena, jis khave man banhe dhiran
> Panjman naun Dharti Mata da lena, jis par kadam takiman
> Chhewan naun Khwaja Pir da lena, jhul pilave thande niran
> Satwan naun Guru Gorakhnath de lena , patal puje bhojan
> Athwan naun lalanwale da lena, bande bande de tabaq janjiran"

Translation
Firstly and lastly, take the name of God; secondly, of the Great Muhammad, the prophet (of God)
Thirdly, take the name of father and mother, on whose milk my body throve
Fourthly, take the name of bread and water, from eating which my heart is gladdened
Fifthly, take the name of Mother Earth, on whom I place my feet.
Sixthly, take the name of Khwaja (Khazir, the Saint), that gives me cold water to drink
Seventhly, take the name of Guru Gorakh Nath whom is worshiped with a platter of milk and rice
Eighthly, take the name of Lalanwala that breaketh the bonds and the chains of the captives

Plot summary

Heer is an extremely beautiful woman, born into a wealthy Jat family of the Sayyal clan in Jhang, Punjab (Pakistan)). Ranjha (whose first name is Dheedo; Ranjha is the surname), also a Jat of the Ranjha clan, is the youngest of four brothers and lives in the village 'Takht Hazara' by the river Chenab. Being his father's favorite son, unlike his brothers who had to toil in the lands, he led a life of ease playing the flute ('Wanjhli'/'Bansuri'). After a quarrel with his brothers over land, Ranjha leaves home. In Waris Shah's version of the epic, it is said that Ranjha left his home because his brothers' wives refused to give him food. Eventually he arrives in Heer's village and falls in love with her. Heer offers Ranjha a job as caretaker of her father's cattle. She becomes mesmerised by the way Ranjha plays his flute and eventually falls in love with him. They meet each other secretly for many years until they are caught by Heer's jealous uncle, Kaido, and her parents Chuchak and Malki. Heer is forced by her family and the local priest or 'mullah' to marry another man called Saida Khera.

Ranjha is heartbroken. He wanders the countrtyside alone, until eventually he meets a 'jogi' (ascetic). After meeting Baba Gorakhnath, the founder of the "Kanphata"(pierced ear) sect of jogis, at 'Tilla Jogian' (the 'Hill of Ascetics', located 50 miles north of the historic town of Bhera, Sargodha District, Punjab), Ranjha becomes a jogi himself, piercing his ears and renouncing the material world. Reciting the name of the Lord, "Alakh Niranjan", he wanders all over the Punjab, eventually finding the village where Heer now lives.

The two return to Heer's village, where Heer's parents agree to their marriage. However, on the wedding day, Heer's jealous uncle Kaido poisons her food so that the wedding will not take place. Hearing this news, Ranjha rushes to aid Heer, but he is too late, as she has already eaten the poison and died. Brokenhearted once again, Ranjha takes the poisoned Laddu (sweet) which Heer has eaten and dies by her side.

Heer and Ranjha are buried in Heer's hometown, Jhang. Lovers and others often pay visits to their mausoleum.

Waris Shah's version

It is believed that the poem of Heer and Ranjha had a happy ending but Waris Shah gave it the sad ending described above, thereby giving it the legendary status it now enjoys. It is argued by Waris Shah in the beginning of his version that the story of Heer and Ranjha has a deeper connotation - the relentless quest of man (humans) for God.

In films

The epic poem has been made into several feature films. Prepartition Indian film versions include *Heer Ranjha* (1928) starring Zubeida, *Heer Ranjha* (1929), *Heer Ranjha* (1931), *Heer Ranjha* (1948). Later Indian versions include the Hindi films *Heer Raanjha* (1971) directed by Chetan Anand and starring Raaj Kumar and Priya Rajvansh, *Heer Ranjha* (1992), and the Punjabi film *Heer Ranjha* (2009) starring singer & actor Harbhajan Mann. Pakistani versions include *Heer Ranjha* (1970) directed by Masood Pervaiz, starring Firdous and Ejaz Durrani with songs by Noor Jehan, *Heer* starring Sowarn Lata and Inayat Hussain Bhatti, and *Heer Sial* starring Sudhir and Bahar.

See also

- Damodar Das Arora
- Mirza Sahiba
- Sassi Punnun
- Sohni Mahiwal

References

- http://www.the-south-asian.com/July-Aug2006/Bhera-PartI-1.htm

External links

- Watch the complete movie Heer Ranjha in Punjabi [1]
- Heer Ranjha Movie Songs [2]
- Complete Heer Waris Shah [3] in Shahmukhi
- About Heer Waris Shah [4]
- Punjabi Literature and Poetry [5] Punjabi Culture and Traditions
- Heer Ranjha OWProject.com [6]
- Google map of Jhang, Pakistan [7]

pnb:□یر رانج□ا

Mirza Sahiba

Mirza Sahiba

Mirza Sahiba (Punjabi: ਮਿਰਜ਼ਾ ਸਾਹਿਬਾਂ, مرزا صاحبا□, *mirzā sāhibāṁ*) is one of the four popular tragic romances of the Punjab. The other three are *Heer Ranjha, Sassi Punnun* and *Sohni Mahiwal.* Mirza Sahiba is one of the classical Punjabi love stories just like Sassi Punnun, Heer Ranjha and Sohni Mahiwal.

Story

Mirza–Sahiba is a treasure of Punjabi literature. It is a romantic tragedy. Sahiba was a love-lorn soul. Shayer Pillo raves about her beauty and says," As Sahiba stepped out with a lungi tied around her waist, the nine angels died on seeing her beauty.

Mirza and Sahiba were childhood playmates and both were born in Jat family , as mentioned in many books and folk tales in punjab,and they fell in love with each other. But when this beauty is about to be wedded forcibly to Tahar Khan by her parents, without any hesitation she sends a taunting message to Mirza, whom she loves, to his village Danabad, through a Brahmin called Kammu.

"You must come and decorate Sahiban's hand with the marriage henna.....

Mirza Khan was the son of Wanjhal Khan, the leader of the Kharal tribe in Danabad, a town in the Jaranwala area of Faisalabad, Pakistan. Sahiba was the daughter of Mahni, the chief of Khewa, a town in Sial Territory in the Jhang district Punjab. Mirza was sent to his relatives' house in Khewa to study, where he met Sahiba and they fell in love. Her family opposed the relationship, and instead arranged a marriage with a member of the Chadhar family.

This is the time you have to protect your self respect and love, keep your promises, and sacrifice your life for truth. Mirza arrived on his horse, Bakki, the night before the wedding and secretly carried her away, planning to elope. Sahiba's brothers got to know about this and decided to follow them. On the way, as Mirza lies under the shade of a tree to rest for a few moments, Sahiba's brothers and chanders caught up with them.

Sahiba was a virtuous and a beautiful soul who did not desire any bloodshed to mar the one she loved. She did not want her hands drenched in blood instead of henna. She knew Mirza was a great archer and he will not miss his target, and if he strikes, her brothers would surely die. Before waking up Mirza, Sahiban breaks his arrows so he can't use them. She presumes on seeing her, her brothers would feel sorry and forgive Mirza and take him in their arms. But the brothers and chanders attack Mirza and kill him. Sahiban takes a sword and slaughters herself and thus bids farewell to this world.

Out of all the legendary stories, Mirza Sahiba's story is the only story where the guy's name comes first and then the girl's. All others start with girl's name for example: Heer Ranjha, Sassi Punnun, Sohni Mahiwal, Laila Majnu. Actually the other folk love stories where the guy's name comes first as (Yousaf khan Sherbano)(Mosa khan Gul maky)(Umar Marvi).

Innumerable folk songs of Punjab narrate the love tale of Sassi and Punnu. The women sing these songs with great emotion and feeling, as though they are paying homage to Sassi with lighted on her tomb. It is not the tragedy of the lovers. It is the co ly believed that the soil of the Punjab has been blessed. God has blessed these lovers. Though their love ended in death, death was a blessing in disguise, for this blessing is immortalized.

Waris shah who sings the tale of Heer elevates mortal love to the same pedestal as spiritual love for God saying," When you start the subject of love, first offer your invocation to God". This has always been the custom in Punjab, where mortal love has been immortalized and enshrined as spirit of love.

Just as every society has dual moral values, so does the Punjabi community. Everything is viewed from two angles, one is a close up of morality and the other is a distant perspective. The social, moral convictions on one hand give poison to Heer and on the other make offerings with spiritual convictions at her tomb, where vows are made and blessings sought for redemption from all sufferings and unfulfilled desires.

But the Sassis, Heers, Sohnis and others born on this soil have revolted against these dual moral standards. The folk songs of Punjab still glorify this rebelliousness.

"When the sheet tear, It can be mended with a patch: How can you darn the torn sky? If the husband dies, another one can be found, But how can one live if the lover dies?"

And perhaps it is the courage of the rebellious Punjabi woman, which has also given her a stupendous sense of perspective. Whenever she asks her lover for a gift she says,

"Get a shirt made for me of the sky And have it trimmed with the earth"

See also

- Heer Ranjha
- Sassi Punnun
- Sohni Mahiwal

External links

- Punjabi Literature and Poetry [5] Punjabi Culture and Traditions

Sohni Mahiwal

Sohni Mahiwal

Sohni Mahiwal (Urdu/Punjabi: سوہنی مہیوال is one of the four popular tragic romances of the Sindh, and Punjab followed by *Heer Ranjha*, *Mirza Sahiba* and *Sassi Punnun*. The story is one of the most prominent examples of medieval poetic legends in the Punjabi, Seraiki and Sindhi languages.

Sohni, the potter's daughter

Sohni was the daughter of a potter named Lula, who lived in Gujarat town (now Dist. Gujarat)in Pakistan, in late Mughal period which is around the 18th century. Sohni's home is now in Punjab (Pakistan). Sohni's shop is situated in Gujrat City Near Rampyari Mahal near the River Chenab where there was a caravan trade route between Bukhara and Delhi.. She helped her father to decorate his pots. As soon as the 'Surahis' (water-pitchers) and mugs came off the wheels, she would draw floral designs on them and transform them into masterpieces of art.

Izzat Baig of Bukhara

Izzat Baig, the rich trader from Bukhara (Uzbekistan), came to India on business and when he saw the beautiful Sohni in the town of Gujarat in Punjab (now Punjab in Pakistan), he was completely enchanted. Instead of keeping 'mohars' (gold coins) in his pockets, he roamed around with his pockets full of love. Just to get a glimpse of Sohni, he would end up buying the water pitchers and mugs everyday.

Sohni lost her heart to Izzat Baig. Instead of making floral designs on earthenware, she started building castles of love in her dreams. Izzat Baig sent off his companions to Bukhara. He took up the job of a servant in the house of Lula, Sohni's father. He would even take their buffaloes for grazing. Soon, he came to be known as "Mahiwal" (buffalo herder).

Sohni's marriage

When the people got to know about the love of Sohni and Mahiwal, without her consent, her parents arranged her marriage with another potter.

Suddenly, one day the "barat" (marriage party) of that potter arrived to her house. Sohni was helpless and in a poignant state. Her parents bundled her off in the "doli" (palanquin), but they could not pack off her love in any doli (box).

Izzat Baig renounced the world and started living like a "faqir" (hermit) in a small hut across the river. The earth of Sohni's land was like a dargah (shrine) for him. He had forgotten his own land, his own people and his world. Taking advantage of the darkness of the night, when the world was fast asleep, Sohni would come by the riverside and Izzat Baig would swim across the river to meet her. He would regularly roast a fish and bring it for her. It is said that once, when due to high tide he could not catch a fish, Mahiwal cut a piece of his thigh and roasted it. Seeing the bandage on his thigh, Sohni opened it, saw the wound and cried.

The end

From the next day, Sohni started swimming across the river with the help of an earthenware pitcher as Izzat Baig was so badly wounded and could not swim across the river. Soon, the rumours of their romantic rendezvous spread. One day Sohni's sister-in-law followed her and saw the hiding place where Sohni used to keep her earthenware pitcher inside the bushes. The next day, the sister-in-law removed the hard baked pitcher and replaced it with an unbaked one. That night, when Sohni tried to cross the river with the help of the pitcher, it dissolved in the water and Sohni drowned in the river. From the other side of the river, Mahiwal saw Sohni drowning and jumped into the river and drowned as well.

Sohni's Tomb

Sohni lies buried in Shahdadpur, Sindh, some 75km from Hyderabad, Pakistan. According to the legend the bodies of Sohni Mahiwal were recovered from the River Indus near this city and hence are buried there.

In Popular Culture

The love story of Sohni and Mahiwal has been the inspiration for numerous songs and poetry in Pakistan, including Pathanay Khan's famous song "Sohni Gharay nu akhadi aj mainu yaar milawa". An Indian film was also made with the name Sohni-Mahiwal(1984) starring Sunny Deol and Poonam Dhillon.

See also

- Heer Ranjha
- Momal Rano
- Sassi Punnun
- LiLa Chanesar
- Noori Jam Tamachi
- Umar Marvi
- Sindhi literature
- Shah Jo Risalo

References

- Sohni & Mehar - The Poetry of Shah [1] (Translated by Elsa Kazi)

Punjabi Kisse

Punjabi Kisse

A **Punjabi qissa** (story; pl. **qisse**) is a tradition of Punjabi language oral story-telling that came to South Asia with migrants from the Arabian peninsula and contemporary Iran and Afghanistan.

Where *qisse* reflect an Islamic and/or Persian heritage of transmitting popular tales of love, valour, honour and moral integrity amongst Muslims, they matured out of the bounds of religion into a more secular form when it reached India and added the existing pre-Islamic Punjabi culture and folklore to its entity.

Etymology

Qisse and the Punjabi culture

The Punjabi language is famous for its rich literature of *qisse*, most of the which are about love, passion, betrayal, sacrifice, social values and a common man's revolt against a larger system. In the Punjabi tradition, friendship, loyalty, love and '*qaul*' (verbal agreement or promise) are given utmost importance and most of the stories in the *qisse* hinge on these critical elements.

Qisse are attributed to have inspired folk music in Punjabi and have added depth and richness to its delivery. These traditions were passed down generations in oral or written forms and were often recited, told as bedtime stories to children or performed musically as folk songs.

Each qissa, if performed, has its unique requirements. A person able to sing or recite one may not necessarily transmit another. The vocal ranges on the musical scale and accurate pauses, if not performed well leaves a performed breathless and unable to continue. Most of the beats used in modern Punjabi music (often misleadingly labelled Bhangra), originated from *qissa* tradition and recitations in old times. *Qisse* also boast to be among the best poetry every written in Punjabi. To date, places like the Qissa Khawani Bazaar (Market of Story-tellers) in Peshawar, Pakistan are thronged by people who visit them to hear oral recitations of *qisse* sung by renowned performers.

Poetry based on *qisse*

Waris Shah's (1722–1798) *qissa* of '*Heer Ranjha*' (formally known as *qissa* '*Heer*') is among the most famous qisse of all times. The effect of *qisse* on Punjabi culture is so strong that even religious leaders and revolutionaries like Guru Gobind Singh and Baba Farid, etc., quoted famous *qisse* in their messages. It will not be wrong to say that popularity and nearly divine status of *qisse* in Punjabi actually inspired many generations of spiritual leaders and social activists to combine the message of God with teenage love tales. This gave rise to what is known as the Sufi movement in Punjab.

The most popular writer/poet to have written Punjabi Sufi *qisse* was Bulleh Shah (c.1680-1758). So popular are his *kalams* (poems) that he is frequently quoted by young and old alike with same respect and on matters of both love and God. In recent times, South Asian singer's have sported these folklores on their albums, for instance, the most famous folklore duo like Kuldeep manak - Dev tharikewala wrote and sang about almost every kissa, and Recently, *Rabbi* by (Rabbi Shergill) contained '*Bulla Ki Jaana Main Kaun*', translated in English as '*I know not who I am*', written by Bulleh Shah. A few years back another singer, (Harbhajan Mann), a Canada-based Punjabi singer rejuvenated the story of '*Sahiba Mirza*', a work by Peelu.

Notable *qisse*

Most of the Punjabi *qisse* were written by Muslim poets who wandered the land. The oldest were usually scripted in Urdu. Some of the most popular *qisse* are listed below.

- '*Mirza Sahiba*' / Peelu
- '*Heer Ranjha*' / Waris Shah
- '*Sohni Mahiwal*' / Hashim Shah
- '*Sassi Punnun*' / Shah Hussain / c.1539–1599
- '*Sucha Singh Soorma*'
- '*Jeona Maur*'
- '*Shirin Farhad*'
- '*Pooran Bhagat*'
- '*Kehar Singh Ram Kaur*'
- '*Sham Kaur/Sham Singh/Sham Lal*'
- '*Dhol Sammi*'
- '*Yusuf Zulekha*'
- '*Kaulan*'
- '*Dulla Bhatti*'
- '*Manu Guggu*'
- '*Ustaad Harman*'
- '*Jatt Parmz*'

References

- Mir, Farina (May 2006). "Genre and Devotion in Punjabi Popular Narratives: Rethinking Cultural and Religious Syncretism". *Comparative Studies in Society and History* (Cambridge University Press) **48** (3): 727–758. doi:10.1017/S0010417506000284 [1].

External links

- ApnaOrg [2] offers one of the most reliable but largely incomplete list of Punjabi literature and music.
- Punjabi People & Old Stories [3] Network of Punjabi People

Sucha Singh Soorma

Sucha Singh Soorma

Sucha Singh is a folk legend (one of the famous Punjabi Kisse) in Punjab, perceived by some as having restored the "family honour" by killing his sister-in-law Balbiro and her alleged extramarital lover Ghukkar, who at one time was his own best friend. Sucha Singh is believed to be of the Jawanda clan.

Balbiro and Ghukkar's Killings

Balbiro's Wedding to Naraina

Balbir Kaur aka Balbiro aka Biro aka Bo was married to a man Juaarh Singh in a village at the border of Patiala-Sangrur. She, the legend has it, poisoned her husband when her husband failed to fulfill her expectations. Having done that, she and her parents invited other marriage proposals,(as you might understand, she would not be expected to be married to a very able person because of her widowhood, given the traditions in Punjab). Having heard about this invitation, Sucha Singh and Ghukkar Mall Chahal, residents of village Samaon near Sangrur, went to see her and spoke to her for Sucha's elder brother Narain Singh.

She accepts the offer for getting married to Naraina on a few conditions. She asks them to load her with jewellery on the wedding, give her freedom in terms of running the house, doing other chores, eating, drinking etc. By the way, she relished drinking liquor and eating meat and chicken. (these as you might again understand were things quite far-fetched to women folk in Punjab). Intending to get Naraina married (he was an addict to opium, as Biro would claim it later), they agree upon all her conditions. Of course she was beautiful too.

Growing Relationship With Ghukkar

After marriage, she was provided with whatever she desired within the families social and financial limits. As Sucha and Ghukkar were very close friends they would often meet up at Sucha's place. As Ghukkar began to frequent his visits, he decided to propose to Balbiro. She was hesitant because of her brother-in-law Sucha but at the same time was attracted to Ghukkar, who was a landlord, a wrestler and an influential person in the village.

Ghukkar's Wily Scheme

As per the scheme, Ghukkar sympathised with Sucha on his financial plight and suggested that they should join the army in Multan. As they go to get recruited, Ghukkar on the pretext of feeling homesick comes back to the village and openly indulged in sex and drunken revelries with Biro.

Sucha Singh's Return

Biro's husband, a submissive person, wrote to Sucha explaining the situation to him. Sucha comes back with the intention of resolving things, conveyed messages to Ghukkar, called upon wiser folk of the village, but Ghukkar did not pay heed or oblige to any instructions. In the meantime, Biro tried to pacify Sucha from taking any extreme step.

Juaan deor de khauf se, paein naar nu haul,
Rafal dunaali vekhke, Biro kare makhaul.

Sucha usually responded by beating her up for bringing this to his house. Biro tried everything, from changing her stance and saying that Ghukkar forced her into doing this --

Biro ro-ro deor nu kahaani dassgi, jaal vich gheri vi bateri fassgi.
Baahle dukh katte nikkal bhambaur se, mallo-malli aanwda ghukkar zor se.

-- to meeting up with Ghukkar to identify a solution, tried to convince her friends to explain it to Sucha that she and Ghukkar were lovers, just like the famous love story "Heer Ranjha", etc, and even threatened Sucha with dire consequences because majority of the village was on Ghukkar's side.

The Showdown

Ghukkar organized a singing programme (Akhara) and on this pretext called upon his various allies from other villages as well.

Nerre-terre baasak nagar Chahalaan de, daru maas veswa patte ve vailaan de,
Chobar bulaale saare deke vaadhi ai, ghukkar pind waale ne sadaale dhadi ai.

Basically, the stage was now set for a face to face confrontation between these one time best friends. The moment came when Biro was passing by and was commented upon by Ghukkar as being his property/possession/mistress. And he asked Biro to come to him and enjoy with him in the company of his friends. Biro obliged. Ghukkar and his friends got drunk and threatened Sucha who prepared himself his rifle and single-handed challenged Ghukkar and his allies to face him in this battle of egos. Ghukkar's allies seeing the weapon and Sucha's high spirits, sheepishly just ran away.

Sihtt jaan chhaviyaan gandaase chhodge, pal vich saare hi yaaraane todge.
Belt gale ch kaartoos sann ge, vekh ke rafal nu hawayiyaan bann ge.

Sucha seeing Ghukkar's friends running for their life, confronted Ghukkar who pleaded for his life. Sucha would not listen, and fired right into Ghukkar from point blank (as they say) after which he killed one of Ghukkar's friends, Bhag Singh, who was brave enough to come back and try to avenge his friends death.

Modhe naal laawe chakk ke machine nu, dabbke stud bhare magazine nu,
Mall vanni chhadde jor-jor shistaan, der na lagawe taahr deve kishtaan.

Filled with rage and vengeance, Sucha then kills his sister-in-law who had in the meantime run home.

Goliyaan de naal bhann sitte pathhe ji, Biro te ghadola digg paein kathhe ji.
Pai geya bhadaaka kaun jhalle sajjno, sarad-sarad goli challe sajjno.

Sucha committing those murders, ran from his village and went west towards Muktsar. Police came really close looking for him, and had some local courageous men rewarded for looking for him. One pathan caught up with Sucha and challenged him. Sucha was the first one to shoot though and kills the pathan too.

Jor leya rafal nu andar khes de, hune naam likh deyaan marabbe es de.

Later Exploits

Murder of Muslim Oppressors

A year passed after the incident in Samaon that Sucha resurfaced again. This time, on his way back to his village to see his brother, he came across an old Hindu woman crying sitting outside her house in a village Bargaadi near Kotkapura. Upon inquiring, he came to know that some Muslims in the village were ill-treating the Hindus, so much so that they stole, slaughtered and feasted on their cattle, while forcing the Hindus to eat it too. Sucha went to the scoundrels and tried to stop them as they were about to kill another cow. This interference infuriated the Muslims who went ahead with the killing anyway. Sucha shot five of them down while a few others managed to run away.

Raaj Kaur's Murder

Later, Sucha joined a group of dacoits and ran havoc in the area. Soon enough, another situation very familiar arose and required his discretion. A widow and a mother of two sons, Raaj Kaur (the elder of the sons, Basant Singh was in his early teens) in village Gehri in Bathinda, started hanging out with another influential man from the same village. Her kids tried to stop her but she would not listen. On the contrary, she got her elder son beaten up by her lover Gajjan Vaili. Basant made contact with his paternal uncle, Ran Singh, who was coincidentally in the army too (just like Sucha). This infuriated Ran but he although had heard the story of Sucha, did not feel he was brave enough to carry out justice there. But he knew that Sucha was around in the area making loots and all. He managed to convey the message to Sucha about the problem his sister-in-law (raaj Kaur) had put his family in. Sucha responded quickly and killed both raaj Kaur and Gajjan Vaili.

Capture of Sucha Singh

Police tracked Sucha down in Kotshamir, a village close to Gehri, after this incident. He was hanged in Gehri in 1911.

Khich lainde phatta jeya lagge na phattka, vajjeya hulaara dhaun khaagi jhatka,
Suche de nikkle praan pal mein, bolke jaikaara tandi paali gal mein.

See also

- Punjabi wedding traditions

References

- Punjabi folk songs and folklore.
- Babu Rajab Ali's take on the legend.

Sanwal Sajal

Sanwal Sajal

Sanwal & Sajal is one of the five popular tragic romances of the Punjab. The other four are *Mirza Sahiba, Sassi Punnun, Sohni Mahiwal & Heer Rangha.* There are several poetic narrations of the story. It tells the story of the love of Sajal and her lover Sanwal.

Sajal is an extremely beautiful woman, born in a *Butt* family. Sanwal (whose first name is Faheem; Sanwal is the nickname) is the oldest of three brothers and lives in the Mohalla "Madan Pura" in a city called Faisalabad. Being his father's favorite son, unlike his brothers who had to toil in the lands, he led a life of ease playing the flute ('Wanjhli'/'Bansuri').

After a quarrel with his brothers over land, Sanwal leaves home. Eventually he arrives in Sajal's village and falls in love with her. Sajal offers Sanwal a job as caretaker of her father's cattle. She becomes mesmerised by the way Sanwal plays his flute and eventually falls in love with him. They meet each other secretly for many years until they are caught by Sanwal's Father.So Sanwal left Sajal's Village and Unfortunately forced by his family and the local priest or *mullah* to marry another girl.

Sajal is shocked.She left the world. and when Sanwal got to know about Sajal's death he was heartbroken. He is left to walk the quiet villages on his own until eventually he meets a *Jogi* (ascetic). After meeting Baba Gorakhnath, the founder of the "*Kanphata*" (pierced ear) sect of ascetics (*Jogis*), at Tilla Jogian (the 'Hill of Ascetics', located 50 miles (80 km) north of the historic town of Bhera, Sargodha District, Punjab (Pakistan)), Sanwal voluntarily becomes a Jogi, piercing his ears and renouncing the material world. Reciting the name of the Lord, "Alakh Niranjan", on his travels around Punjab and eventually, one day, finds the village where he is reunited with Sajal.

Punjabi folklore

Punjabi folklore

Punjabi folklore is the body of expressive culture, including tales, music, dance, legends, oral history, proverbs, jokes, popular beliefs, customs of Punjabi people.

Punjabi Folklore, particularly its folksongs, are said to be the "autobiography of its people".

See also

- Punjabi wedding traditions
- Folklore

External links

- Punjabi Folksongs [1]

Sassi Punnun

Sassi Punnun

Sassui Punnun (or *Sassui Panhu* or *Sassui Punhun*) ({{Sindhi/Punjabi:سَسئي پُنهوُن}},Urdu: سسی پنو); is one of the seven popular tragic romances of the Sindh and four of the most popular in Punjab. The other six are *Umar Marvi*, *Momal Rano* and *Sohni Mahiwal*, *Laila Chanesar*, *Sorath Rai Diyach*, *Noori Jam Tamachi* commonly known as Seven Queens (Sindhi: ست مورميون) of Shah Abdul Latif Bhittai . Sassui Punnun was written by the Sindhi and Sufi poet, Shah Abdul Latif Bhittai in (1689–1752). Regionally this unforgettable Romance happened in the region of Balochistan district Turbat, Pakistan.

Makran Coastal Highway

The Makran Coastal Highway is located in Balochistan, Pakistan. As we drive along the Makran Coastal Highway we can see The fort of Sassi Punno whose construction dates back to 600 to 800 BC. It is widely believed that the P]]transformed into a figure made out of stone. One interesting feature of the figure is that her visage is facing Kech Turbat, the region where Punno

Sassi

Sassi was the daughter of the *'King of Bhambour* in Sindh, Pakistan. Upon Sassi's birth, astrologers predicted that she was a curse for the royal family's prestige. The King ordered that the child be put in a wooden box and thrown in the river Indus. A washerman of the Bhambour village found the wooden box and the child in the box. The washerman believed the child was a blessing from God and took her home. As he had no child of his own, he decided to adopt her.Sussi is also known as the princess of hope.

Sassi and Punnu meet

When Sassi became a young girl, she was as beautiful as the fairies of heaven. Stories of her beauty reached Punnun and he became desperate to meet Sassi. The handsome young Prince of Makran therefore travelled to Bhambour. He sent his clothes to Sassi's father (a washerman) so that he could catch a glimpse of Sassi. When he visited the washerman's house, they fell in love at first sight. Sassi's father was dispirited, hoping that Sassi would marry a washerman and no one else. Sassi's father asked Punnun to prove that he was worthy of Sassi by passing the test as a washerman. Punnun agreed to prove his love. While washing, he tore all the clothes as, being a prince, he had never washed any clothes; he thus failed the agreement. But before he returned those clothes, he hid gold coins in the pockets of all the clothes, hoping this would keep the villagers quiet. The trick worked, and Sassi's father agreed to the marriage.

Punnun's brothers

Punnun's father and brothers were against his marriage to Sassi (Punnun being a prince and she being a washerman's daughter), and so, for their father's sake, Punnun's brothers traveled to Bhambhor. First they threatened Punnun but when he didn't relent, they tried more devious methods.

Punnun was surprised to see his brothers supporting his marriage and on the first night, they pretended to enjoy and participate in the marriage celebrations and forced Punnun to drink different types of wines. When he was intoxicated they carried him on a camel's back and returned to their hometown of Kicham.

The lovers meet their end

The next morning, when Sassi realized that she was cheated, she became mad with the grief of separation from her lover and ran barefoot towards the town of Kicham. To reach it, she had to cross miles of desert. Alone, she continued her journey until her feet were blistered and her lips were parched from crying "Punnun, Punnun!". The journey was full of dangerous hazards, which lead to her demise. Punnun's name was on Sassi's lips throughout the journey. She was thirsty, there she saw a shepherd coming out of a hut. He gave her some water to drink. Seeing her incredible beauty, dirty lustful thoughts came into his mind, and he tried to force himself on Sassi. Sassi ran away and prayed to God to hide her and when God listened to her prayers, land shook and split and Sassi found herself buried in the valley of mountains. When Punnun woke he was himself in Makran he could not stop himself from running back to Bhambhor. On the way he called out "Sassi, Sassi!" to which the shepherd replied. The shepherd told Punnun the whole story. Then Punnun also lamented the same prayer, the land shook and split again and he was also buried in the same mountain valley as Sassi. The legendary grave still exists in this valley. Shah Abdul Latif Bhittai sings this historic tale in his sufi poetry as an example of eternal love and union with Divine.

See also

- LiLa Chanesar
- Heer Ranjha
- Momal Rano
- Umar Marvi
- Sohni Mahiwal
- Noori Jam Tamachi
- Sindhi literature
- Shah Abdul Latif Bhittai

References

- [1](Sassi and Punnu (Sindh))
- [2]
- [3]

pnb:سسی پنوں

Dhaj, Ror Kumar

Dhaj, Ror Kumar

Raja Dhaj or **Rai Diyach**, a name by which he is better known among Sindhi Rajputs when they listen to the ballad of Sorath, is an ancient figure made immortal by his abduction of Sorath, a woman of legendary beauty. His deeds are still recounted after hundreds of years in the states of Haryana (the highly popular swaang called Sorath), Rajasthan, Gujarat and Sindh (Sur Sorath, one of the traditional 30 Surs included in Shah Jo Risalo). *Sorath - Rai Diyach* is one of the seven popular tragic romances of the Sindh, the other six being Umar Marvi, Momal Rano, Sohni Mahiwal, Laila Chanesar, Sassui Punnun, Noori Jam Tamachi. Together, they are commonly known as Seven Queens (Sindhi: مورميون ست) of Shah Abdul Latif Bhittai.

The story of the abduction of Sorath by Dhaj, Ror Kumar has been portrayed by swaang artistes in Haryana and Rajasthan since times immemorial. In Sindh, it was penned down by the Sindhi Sufi poet, Shah Abdul Latif Bhittai during his lifetime, 1689-1752, based on pre-existing legends. This unforgettable romance is based on actual history that has to do with the times of the founder of Rori Shankar in Sindh, who was none other than the protagonist of this story. With the establishment of Rori, Dhaj, Ror Kumar founded the Ror Dynasty, which was to rule Sindh for the next one thousand years, in 450 BC.

Historical importance

Historian Dr. Raj Pal Singh, a Jat by caste himself, has said in his book "Ror itihaas ki jhalak",

> Raja Dhaj occupies an extremely important place in the history of Rors. His name is commonly on the tip of every Ror's tongue and he has become the popular subject of many swaang episodes and songs, which are heard with great admiration by people of all castes in North India even today.

Progeny

Dhaj, Ror Kumar had six sons from Sorath. They were named as Kunak, Takshak, Prasenjit, Kardhman, Raghu and Sharanjit. Kunak succeeded Raja Dhaj as the monarch of Sindh and Hind; Takshak went to Lucknow, Raghu went to the present-day Pune-Satara area, Prasenjit renounced the world and became a *Jogi*; Kardhman went to Eastern Uttar Pradesh and his descendants are supposed to be the owners of 84 villages in the present-day Gorakhpur and Gonda districts till today.

See also

- Shah Abdul Latif Bhittai
- Ror
- Ror Dynasty

References

- A part of Bhittai's "Sur Sorath" [1]
- The full story of Dhaj, Ror Kumar and Sorath, which has been compiled by Shri Ramdas after consulting swaang artistes as well as bards, can be read in the book "Aryavart evam Ror Vansh ka itihaas" on pages 68-98

Shahrukh Husain

Shahrukh Husain

Shahrukh Husain (Urdu: شا□ رخ حسین), born 28 April 1950, is an author of Pakistani origin who specializes in fiction, non-fiction, and screenwriting. She is also a psychotherapist, folklorist, and storyteller. She currently resides in London.

Select filmography

- Screenplay for *In Custody* (1993), adapted from the novel of the same name by Anita Desai. It is a Merchant Ivory Productions film directed by Ismail Merchant.

Select books

- *The Goddess: Power, Sexuality, and the Feminine Divine* (2003)
- *Daughters of the Moon: Witch Tales from Around the World* (1993)
- *Handsome Heroines* (1996).

External links

- Royal Literary Fund biography [1]
- Biography from Barefoot Books [2]
- Penguin biography [3]
- Interview with writewords.org [4]

Jinn

Jinn

Jinn (Arabic: جني *jinnī*; variant spelling *djinni*) or **genie** is a supernatural creature in Arab folklore and Islamic teachings which occupies a parallel world to that of mankind. Together, jinn, humans and angels make up the three sentient creations of Allah. According to the Qur'ān, there are two creations that have free will: humans and jinn. Religious sources say little about them; however, the Qur'an mentions that Jinn are made of smokeless flame or "the fire of a scorching wind". They have the ability to change their shape. Like human beings, the jinn can also be good, evil, or neutrally benevolent.

The Majlis al-Jinn cave in Oman, literally "Meeting place of the Jinn".

The Jinn are mentioned frequently in the Qur'an, and there is a surah entitled Sūrat al-Jinn in the Quran. Islamic scholars have ruled that it is apostasy to disbelieve in one of Allah's creations. Some research by the American Jewish Committee has shown that the belief in jinn has fallen compared to the belief in angels in other Abrahamic traditions.

Etymology and definitions

Jinn is a word of the collective number in Arabic, derived from the Arabic root *j-n-n* meaning 'to hide' or 'be hidden'. Other words derived from this root are *majnūn* 'mad' (literally, 'one whose intellect is hidden'), *junūn* 'madness', and *janīn* 'embryo, fetus' ('hidden inside the womb').

The Arabic root *j-n-n* means 'to hide, conceal'. A word for garden or Paradise, جنّة *jannah*, is a cognate of the Hebrew word גן *gan* 'garden', derived from the same Semitic root. In arid climates, gardens have to be protected against desertification by walls; this is the same concept as in the word *paradise* from *pairi-daêza*, an Avestan word for garden that literally means 'having walls built around'. Thus the protection of a garden behind walls implies its being hidden from the outside. Arabic lexicons such as Edward William Lane's *Arabic-English Lexicon* define *jinn* not only as spirits, but also anything concealed through time, status, and even physical darkness.

The word *genie* in English is derived from Latin *genius*, which meant a sort of tutelary or guardian spirit thought to be assigned to each person at their birth. English borrowed the French descendant of this word, *génie*; its earliest written attestation in English, in 1655, is a plural spelled "genyes." The French translators of *The Book of One Thousand and One Nights* used *génie* as a translation of *jinnī* because it was similar to the Arabic word in sound and in meaning. This use was also adopted in English and has since become dominant.

Existence and usage of genie in other culture

Jinn in the pre-Islamic era

Amongst archaeologists dealing with ancient Middle Eastern cultures, any spirit lesser than angels is often referred to as a *jinni*, especially when describing stone carvings or other forms of art.

Inscriptions found in Northwestern Arabia seem to indicate the worship of jinn, or at least their tributary status. For instance, an inscription from Beth Fasi'el near Palmyra pays tribute to the "*Jinnaye*", the "good and rewarding gods".

In the following verse, the Quran vehemently rejects the worship of Jinn and stresses that only God should be worshiped:

"*Yet they make the jinns equals with Allah, though Allah did create the jinns; and they falsely, having no knowledge, attribute to Him sons and daughters. Praise and glory be to Him! (for He is) above what they attribute to Him!*" (Quran 6:100)

Types of jinn include the *shayṭān*, the *ghūl*, the *marīd*, the *'ifrīt*, and the *jinn*. According to the information in the Arabian Nights, 'ifrits seem to be the strongest form of jinn, followed by marids, and then the rest of the jinn forms.

Genie in Islam

In Islamic theology jinn are said to be creatures with free will, made from smokeless fire by Allah as humans were made of clay. According to the Qur'an, jinn have free will, and Iblis abused this freedom in front of Allah by refusing to bow to Adam when Allah ordered angels and jinn to do so. For disobeying Allah, he was expelled from Paradise and called "*Shayṭān*" (Satan). Jinn are frequently mentioned in the Qur'an: Surah 72 (named *Sūrat al-Jinn*) is named after the jinn, and has a passage about them. Another surah (*Sūrat al-Nās*) mentions jinn in the last verse. The Qur'an also mentions that Muhammad was sent as a prophet to both "humanity and the jinn," and that prophets and messengers were sent to both communities.

Similar to humans, jinn have free will allowing them to do as they choose (such as follow any religion). They are usually invisible to humans, and humans do not appear clearly to them. Jinn have the power to travel large distances at extreme speeds and are thought to live in remote areas, mountains, seas, trees, and the air, in their own communities. Like humans, jinn will also be judged on the Day of Judgment and will be sent to Paradise or Hell according to their deeds.

Classifications and characteristics

The social organization of the jinn community resembles that of humans; e.g., they have kings, courts of law, weddings, and mourning rituals. A few traditions (hadith), divide jinn into three classes: those who have wings and fly in the air, those who resemble snakes and dogs, and those who travel about ceaselessly. Other reports claim that ʻAbd Allāh ibn Masʻūd (d. 652), who was accompanying Muhammad when the jinn came to hear his recitation of the Qur'an, described them as creatures of different forms; some resembling vultures and snakes, others tall men in white garb. They may even appear as dragons, onagers, or a number of other animals. In addition to their animal forms, the jinn occasionally assume human form to mislead and destroy their human victims. Certain hadiths have also claimed that the jinn may subsist on bones, which will grow flesh again as soon as they touch them, and that their animals may live on dung, which will revert to grain or grass for the use of the jinn flocks.

Ibn Taymiyyah believed the jinn were generally "ignorant, untruthful, oppressive and treacherous".

Ibn Taymiyyah believes that the jinn account for much of the "magic" perceived by humans, cooperating with magicians to lift items in the air unseen, delivering hidden truths to fortune tellers, and mimicking the voices of deceased humans during seances.

In the following verse of the Quran, it is affirmed that prophets were sent to the Jinn as they were sent to men.

"*O ye assembly of jinns and men! came there not unto you apostles from amongst you, setting forth unto you My signs, and warning you of the meeting of this Day of yours (The Day of Judgment)?" They will say: "We bear witness against ourselves." It was the life of this world that deceived them. So against themselves will they bear witness that they rejected Faith.*" (Quran 6:130)

Qarīn

A related belief is that every person is assigned one's own special jinnī, also called a *qarīn*, of the jinn that whisper to people's souls and tell them to submit to evil desires. However, the notion of a *qarīn* is not universally accepted amongst all Muslims. But it is generally accepted that Shayṭān whispers in human minds, and he is assigned to each human being.

Relationship of King Solomon and the genies

See main article Islamic view of Solomon

According to traditions, the jinn stood behind the learned humans in Solomon's court, who in turn, sat behind the prophets. The jinn remained in the service of Solomon, who had placed them in bondage, and had ordered them to perform a number of tasks.

"*...and there were jinns that worked in front of him, by the leave of his Lord,*" (Quran 13:12)

"*And before Solomon were marshalled his hosts,- of jinns and men and birds, and they were all kept in order and ranks.*" (Quran 27:17)

The Qur'an relates that Solomon died while he was leaning on his staff. As he remained upright, propped on his staff, the jinn thought he was still alive and supervising them, so they continued to work. They realized the truth only when God sent a creature to crawl out of the ground and gnaw at Solomon's staff until his body collapsed. The Qur'an then comments that if they had known the unseen, they would not have stayed in the humiliating torment of being enslaved.

"*Then, when We decreed (Solomon's) death, nothing showed them his death except a little worm of the earth, which kept (slowly) gnawing away at his staff: so when he fell down, the jinns saw plainly that if they had known the unseen, they would not have tarried in the humiliating Penalty (of their Task).*" Quran 34:14)

Esoteric theories

In 1998, Pakistani nuclear scientist Sultan Bashiruddin Mahmood proposed in a Wall Street Journal interview that jinn (described in the Qur'ān as beings made of fire) could be tapped to solve the energy crisis. "I think that if we develop our souls, we can develop communication with them. ... Every new idea has its opponents, but there is no reason for this controversy over Islam and science because there is no conflict between Islam and science."

See also

- Jinn in popular culture
- Christian demonology
- 'Ifrīt, class of jinn that live in abandoned buildings
- Marīd, class of jinn associated with the sea
- Elf
- Fairy

References

- Al-Ashqar, Dr. Umar Sulaiman (1998). *The World of the Jinn and Devils*. Boulder, CO: Al-Basheer Company for Publications and Translations.
- Barnhart, Robert K. *The Barnhart Concise Dictionary of Etymology*. 1995.
- "Genie". *The Oxford English Dictionary*. Second edition, 1989.
- Abu al-Futūḥ Rāzī, *Tafsīr-e rawḥ al-jenān va rūḥ al-janān* IX-XVII (pub. so far), Tehran, 1988.
- Moḥammad Ayyūb Ṭabarī, *Tuḥfat al-gharā'ib*, ed. J. Matīnī, Tehran, 1971.
- A. Aarne and S. Thompson, *The Types of the Folktale*, 2nd rev. ed., Folklore Fellows Communications 184, Helsinky, 1973.
- Abu'l-Moayyad Balkhī, *Ajā'eb al-donyā*, ed. L. P. Smynova, Moscow, 1993.
- A. Christensen, *Essai sur la Demonologie iranienne*, Det. Kgl. Danske Videnskabernes Selskab, Historisk-filologiske Meddelelser, 1941.
- R. Dozy, *Supplément aux Dictionnaires arabes*, 3rd ed., Leyden, 1967.
- H. El-Shamy, *Folk Traditions of the Arab World: A Guide to Motif Classification*, 2 vols., Bloomington, 1995.
- Abū Bakr Moṭahhar Jamālī Yazdī, *Farrokh-nāma*, ed. Ī. Afshār, Tehran, 1967.
- Abū Jaʿfar Moḥammad Kolaynī, *Ketāb al-kāfī*, ed. A. Ghaffārī, 8 vols., Tehran, 1988.
- Edward William Lane, *An Arabic-English Lexicon* [1], Beirut, 1968.
- L. Loeffler, *Islam in Practice: Religious Beliefs in a Persian Village*, New York, 1988.
- U. Marzolph, *Typologie des persischen Volksmärchens*, Beirut, 1984. Massé, Croyances.
- M. Mīhandūst, *Padīdahā-ye wahmī-e dīrsāl dar janūb-e Khorāsān*, Honar o mordom, 1976, pp. 44–51.
- T. Nöldeke "Arabs (Ancient)," in J. Hastings, ed., *Encyclopaedia of Religion and Ethics* I, Edinburgh, 1913, pp. 659–73.
- S. Thompson, *Motif-Index of Folk-Literature*, rev. ed., 6 vols., Bloomington, 1955.
- S. Thompson and W. Roberts, *Types of Indic Oral Tales*, Folklore Fellows Communications 180, Helsinki, 1960.
- Solṭān-Moḥammad ibn Tāj al-Dīn Ḥasan Esterābādī, *Toḥfat al-majāles*, Tehran,
- Moḥammad b. Maḥmūd Ṭūsī, *Ajāyeb al-makhlūqāt va gharā'eb al-mawjūdāt*, ed. M. Sotūda, Tehran, 1966.

Further reading

- Crapanzano, V. (1973) *The Hamadsha: a study in Moroccan ethnopsychiatry*. Berkeley, CA, University of California Press.
- Drijvers, H. J. W. (1976) *The Religion of Palmyra*. Leiden, Brill.
- El-Zein, Amira (2009) *Islam, Arabs, and the intelligent world of the Jinn*. Contemporary Issues in the Middle East. Syracuse, NY, Syracuse University Press. ISBN 978-0-8156-3200-9
- El-Zein, Amira (2006) "Jinn". In: J. F. Meri ed. *Medieval Islamic civilization – an encyclopedia*. New York and Abingdon, Routledge, pp. 420–421.
- Goodman, L.E. (1978) *The case of the animals versus man before the king of the Jinn: A tenth–century ecological fable of the pure brethren of Basra*. Library of Classical Arabic Literature, vol. 3. Boston, Twayne.
- Maarouf, M. (2007) *Jinn eviction as a discourse of power: a multidisciplinary approach to Moroccan magical beliefs and practices*. Leiden, Brill.
- Zbinden, E. (1953) *Die Djinn des Islam und der altorientalische Geisterglaube*. Bern, Haupt.

External links

- Etymology of *genie* [2]
- Visions of the Jinn – a Muslim scholar's experience with Jinn [3]
- Sūrat al-Jinn from the Qur'ān [4]
- What are Jinns and Spirits ? [5]

ckb:جن

One Thousand and One Nights

One Thousand and One Nights

Queen Scheherazade tells her stories to King Shahryār.

Arab World
This article is part of the series: **Arab Culture**

One Thousand and One Nights (Arabic: كتاب ألف ليلة وليلة *Kitāb 'alf layla wa-layla*; Persian: هزار و یک شب *Hezār-o yek šab*) is a collection of Middle Eastern and South Asian stories and folk tales compiled in Arabic during the Islamic Golden Age. It is often known in English as the ***Arabian Nights***, from the first English language edition (1706), which rendered the title as *The Arabian Nights' Entertainment*.

The work as we have it was collected over many centuries by various authors, translators and scholars across the Middle East and North Africa. The tales themselves trace their roots back to ancient and medieval Arabic, Persian, Indian, Egyptian and Mesopotamian folklore and literature. In particular, many tales were originally folk stories from the Caliphate era, while others, especially the frame story, are most probably drawn from the Pahlavi Persian work *Hezār Afsān* (Persian: هزار افسان, lit. *A Thousand Tales*) which in turn relied partly on Indian elements. Though the oldest Arabic manuscript dates from the 14th century, scholarship generally dates the collection's genesis to around the 9th century.

What is common throughout all the editions of the *Nights* is the initial frame story of the ruler Shahryar (from Persian: شهریار, meaning "king" or "sovereign") and his wife Scheherazade (from Persian: شهرزاده, possibly meaning "of noble lineage") and the framing device incorporated throughout the tales themselves. The stories proceed from this original tale; some are framed within other tales, while others begin and end of their own accord. Some editions contain only a few hundred nights, while others include 1,001 or more.

Some of the best-known stories of *The Nights*, particularly "Aladdin's Wonderful Lamp", "Ali Baba and the Forty Thieves" and "The Seven Voyages of Sinbad the Sailor", while almost certainly genuine Middle-Eastern folk tales, were not part of *The Nights* in Arabic versions, but were interpolated into the collection by Antoine Galland and other European translators.

Synopsis

See also: List of stories within One Thousand and One Nights and List of characters within One Thousand and One Nights

The main frame story concerns a Persian king and his new bride. He is shocked to discover that his brother's wife is unfaithful; discovering his own wife's infidelity has been even more flagrant, he has her executed: but in his bitterness and grief decides that all women are the same. The king, Shahryar, begins to marry a succession of virgins only to execute each one the next morning, before she has a chance to dishonour him. Eventually the vizier, whose duty it is to provide them, cannot find any more virgins. Scheherazade, the vizier's daughter, offers herself as the next bride and her father reluctantly agrees. On the night of their marriage, Scheherazade begins to tell the king a tale, but does not end it. The king is thus forced to postpone her execution in order to hear the conclusion. The next night, as soon as she finishes the tale, she begins (and *only* begins) a new one, and the king, eager to hear the conclusion, postpones her execution once again. So it goes on for 1,001 nights.

The tales vary widely: they include historical tales, love stories, tragedies, comedies, poems, burlesques and various forms of erotica. Numerous stories depict djinn, magicians, and legendary places, which are often intermingled with real people and geography, not always rationally; common protagonists include the historical caliph Harun al-Rashid, his vizier, Ja'far al-Barmaki, and his alleged court poet Abu Nuwas, despite the fact that these figures lived some 200 years after the fall of the Sassanid Empire in which the frame tale of Scheherazade is set. Sometimes a character in Scheherazade's tale will begin telling other characters a story of his own, and that story may have another one told within it, resulting in a richly layered narrative texture.

The different versions have different individually detailed endings (in some Scheherazade asks for a pardon, in some the king sees their children and decides not to execute his wife, in some other things happen that make the king distracted) but they all end with the king giving his wife a pardon and sparing her life.

The narrator's standards for what constitutes a cliffhanger seem broader than in modern literature. While in many cases a story is cut off with the hero in danger of losing his life or another kind of deep trouble, in some parts of the full text Scheherazade stops her narration in the middle of an exposition of abstract philosophical principles or complex points of Islamic philosophy, and in one case during a detailed description of human anatomy according to Galen—and in all these cases turns out to be justified in her belief that the king's curiosity about the sequel would buy her another day of life.

History and editions

"The Sultan Pardons Scheherazade", by Arthur Boyd Houghton (1836–1875)

Early influences

The tales in the collection can be traced to Arabic, Egyptian, Persian and Indian storytelling traditions of ancient and medieval times. Many stories from Indian and Persian folklore parallel the tales as well as Jewish sources. These tales were probably in circulation before they were collected and codified into a single collection. This work was further shaped by scribes, storytellers, and scholars and evolved into a collection of three distinct layers of storytelling by the 15th century:

A page from *Kelileh va Demneh* dated 1429, from Herat, a Persian translation of the *Panchatantra* — depicts the manipulative jackal-vizier, Dimna, trying to lead his lion-king into war.

1. Persian tales influenced by Indian folklore and adapted into Arabic by the 10th century.
2. Stories recorded in Baghdad during the 10th century.
3. Medieval Egyptian folklore.

Indian folklore is represented by certain animal stories, which reflect influence from ancient Sanskrit fables. The influence of the *Panchatantra* and *Baital Pachisi* are particularly notable. *The Jataka Tales* are a collection of 547 Buddhist stories, which are for the most part moral stories with an ethical purpose. *The Tale of the Bull and the Ass* and the linked *Tale of the Merchant and his Wife* are found in the frame stories of both the *Jataka* and the *Nights.*

The influence of the folklore of Baghdad is represented by the tales of the Abbasid caliphs; the Cairene influence is made evident by *Maruf the cobbler.* Tales such as *Iram of the columns* are based upon the pre-Islamic legends of the Arabian Peninsula; motifs are employed from the ancient Mesopotamian tale, the *Epic of Gilgamesh.* There is also a Shia Muslim influence. Possible Greek influences have also been noted.

Versions

Early references to the collection are found in the writings of Masudi (d.956), who mentions it as a translated book full of untrue stories, and of bookseller Ibn al-Nadim (987–88), who also describes it disparagingly as a "coarse book" and retells the frame story about Shahryar and Scheherazade. In the earliest mentions, the book was referred to variously with the Persian title *Hazār Afsān* "A Thousand Tales" and with the popular Arabic name *Alf Layla* "A Thousand Nights"; the name "One Thousand and One Nights" is first attested in a 12th century loan record for a Jewish bookseller in Cairo. However, while this and other evidence suggests that the book was popular during that time and later, the earliest substantial manuscripts that are still preserved today date only from the 14th and 15th centuries. Two main Arabic manuscript traditions of the Nights are known – the Syrian and the

Egyptian.

The Syrian tradition includes the oldest manuscripts; these versions are also much shorter and include fewer tales. It is represented in print by the so-called *Calcutta I* (1814–1818) and most notably by the *Leiden edition* (1984), which is based above all on the *Galland manuscript*. It is believed to be the purest expression of the style of the mediaeval *Arabian Nights*.

Texts of the Egyptian tradition emerge later and contain many more tales of much more varied content; a much larger number of originally independent tales have been incorporated into the collection over the centuries, most of them after the Galland manuscript was written, and were being included as late as in the 18th and 19th centuries, perhaps in order to attain the eponymous number of 1001 nights. The final product of this tradition, the so-called Zotenberg Egyptian Recension, does contain 1001 nights and is reflected in print, with slight variations, by the editions known as the *Bulaq* (1835) and the *Macnaghten* or *Calcutta II* (1839–1842).

All extant substantial versions of both recensions share a small common core of tales, namely:

- The Merchant and the Demon.
- The Fisherman and the Jinni.
- The Story of the Porter and the Three Ladies.
- The Hunchback cycle.
- The Story of the Three Apples, enframing the Story of Nur al-Din and Shams al-Din
- The Story of Nur al-Din Ali and Anis al-Jalis
- The Story of Ali Ibn Baqqar and Shams al-Nahar, and
- The Story of Qamar al-Zaman.

The texts of the Syrian recension don't contain much beside that core. It is debated which of the Arabic recensions is more "authentic" and closer to the original: the Egyptian ones have been modified more extensively and more recently, and scholars such as Muhsin Mahdi have suspected that this may have been caused in part by European demand for a "complete version"; but it appears that this type of modification has been common throughout the history of the collection, and independent tales have always been added to it.

The first European version (1704–1717) was translated into French by Antoine Galland from an Arabic text of the Syrian recension and other sources. This 12-volume book, *Les Mille et une nuits, contes arabes traduits en français* ("Thousand and one nights, Arab stories translated into French"), included stories that were not in the original Arabic manuscript. "Aladdin's Lamp" and "Ali Baba and the Forty Thieves" appeared first in Galland's translation and cannot be found in any of the original manuscripts. He wrote that he heard them from a Syrian Christian storyteller from Aleppo, a Maronite scholar whom he called "Hanna Diab." Galland's version of the *Nights* was immensely popular throughout Europe, and later versions were issued by Galland's publisher using Galland's name without his consent.

As scholars were looking for the presumed "complete" and "original" form of the Nights, they naturally turned to the more voluminous texts of the Egyptian recension, which soon came to be viewed as the "standard version". The first translations of this kind, such as that of Edward Lane (1840, 1859), were bowdlerized. Unabridged and unexpurgated translations were made, first by John Payne, under the title *The Book of the Thousand Nights and One Night* (1882, nine volumes), and then by Sir Richard Francis Burton, entitled *The Book of the Thousand Nights and a Night* (1885, ten volumes) – the latter was, according to some assessments, partially based on the former, leading to charges of plagiarism. In view of the sexual imagery in the source texts (which Burton even emphasized further, especially by adding extensive footnotes and appendices on Oriental sexual mores) and the strict Victorian laws on obscene material, both of these translations were printed as private editions for subscribers only, rather than published in the usual manner. Burton's original 10 volumes were followed by a further six entitled *The Supplemental Nights to the Thousand Nights and a Night*, which were printed between 1886 and 1888. Burton's edition is the more famous one; taken together with the Supplements, it is still valued as "the most complete version of texts relating to the Arabian nights available in English". It has, however, been severely criticized for its "archaic language and extravagant idiom" and "obsessive focus on sexuality" (and has even been condemned as an "eccentric ego-trip" and a "highly personal reworking of the text").

Poster for a Russian production of 1001 nights.

Later versions of the *Nights* include that of the French doctor J. C. Mardrus, issued from 1898 to 1904. It was translated into English by Powys Mathers, and issued in 1923. Like Payne's and Burton's texts, it is based on the Egyptian recension and retains the erotic material, indeed expanding on it, but it has been criticized for inaccuracy.

A notable recent version, which reverts to the Syrian recension, is a critical edition based on the 14th or 15th century Syrian manuscript in the Bibliothèque Nationale, originally used by Galland. This version, known as the Leiden text, was compiled in Arabic by Muhsin Mahdi (1984) and rendered into English by Husain Haddawy (1990). Mahdi argued that this version is the earliest extant one (a view that is largely accepted today) and that it reflects most closely a "definitive" coherent text ancestral to all others that he believed to have existed during the Mamluk period (a view that remains contentious). Still, even scholars who deny this version the exclusive status of "the only *real* Arabian Nights" recognize it as being the best source on the original *style* and linguistic form of the mediaeval work and praise the Haddawy translation as "very readable" and "strongly recommended for anyone who wishes to taste the authentic flavour of those tales". An additional second volume of *Arabian nights* translated by Haddawy, composed of popular tales *not* present in the Leiden edition, was published in 1995.

In 2008 a new English translation was published by Penguin Classics in three volumes. It is translated by Malcolm C. Lyons and Ursula Lyons with introduction and annotations by Robert Irwin. This is the first "complete" translation of the Macnaghten or Calcutta II edition (Egyptian recension) since Sir Richard Burton. It contains, in addition to the standard text of 1001 Nights, the so-called "orphan stories" of *Aladdin* and *Ali Baba* as well as an alternative ending to *The seventh journey of Sindbad* from Antoine Galland's original French. Unfortunately, the Lyons translation is not truly complete. As the translator himself notes in his preface to the three volumes, it is a "streamlined" version, "more for the eye than the ear." Thus much material has been omitted, and this could be considered regrettable.

In 2005, Brazilian scholar Mamede Mustafa Jarouche started publishing a thorough Portuguese translation of the work, based on the comparative analysis of a series of different Arabic manuscripts. The first three volumes of a planned five- or six-volume set have already been released, comprising the complete Syrian branch of the book (volumes 1 and 2) and part of the later Egyptian branch (volume 3 and onwards).

Timeline

Scholars have assembled a timeline concerning the publication history of *The Nights*:

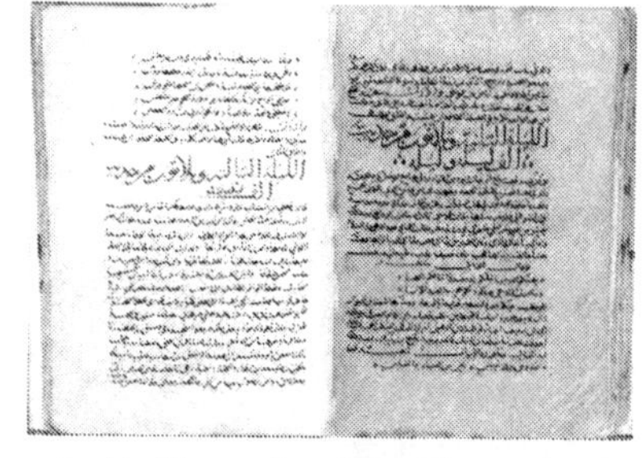

Arabic Manuscript of The Thousand and One Nights dating back to the 1300s

- Oldest Arabic manuscript fragment (a few handwritten pages) from Syria dating to the early 9th century discovered by scholar Nabia Abbott in 1948.
- 10th century — Mention of *The Nights* in Ibn Al-Nadim's "Fihrist" (Catalogue of books) in Baghdad. He mentions the book's history and its Persian origins.
- 10th century — Second oldest reference to *The Nights* in Muruj Al-Dhahab (The Meadows of Gold) by Al-Masudi.
- 11th century — Mention of *The Nights* by Qatran Tabrizi in the following couplet in Persian:

هزار ره صفت هفت خوان و رویین دژ
هزار افسان فرو شنیدم و خواندم من از

A thousand times, accounts of *Rouyin Dezh* and *Haft Khān*
I heard and read from *Hezār Afsān* (literally Thousand Fables)

- 14th century — Existing Syrian manuscript in the Bibliothèque Nationale in Paris (contains about 300 tales).
- 1704 — Antoine Galland's French translation is the first European version of *The Nights*. Later volumes were introduced using Galland's name though the stories were written by unknown persons

at the behest of the publisher wanting to capitalize on the popularity of the collection.

- 1706 — An anonymously translated version in English appears in Europe dubbed the "Grub Street" version. This is entitled *The Arabian Nights' Entertainment* - the first known use of the common English title of the work.
- 1714 — *The Thousand and One Days: Persian Tales* by Ambrose Philips. The earliest English translation with an attributed author.
- 1775 — Egyptian version of *The Nights* called "ZER" (Hermann Zotenberg's Egyptian Recension) with 200 tales (no surviving edition exists).
- 1814 — Calcutta I, the earliest existing Arabic printed version, is published by the British East India Company. A second volume was released in 1818. Both had 100 tales each.
- 1825–1838 — The Breslau/Habicht edition is published in Arabic in 8 volumes. Christian Maxmilian Habicht (born in Breslau, Germany, 1775) collaborated with the Tunisian Murad Al-Najjar and created this edition containing 1001 stories. Using versions of *The Nights*, tales from Al-Najjar, and other stories from unknown origins Habicht published his version in Arabic and German.
- 1842–1843 — Four additional volumes by Habicht.
- 1835 Bulaq version — These two volumes, printed by the Egyptian government, are the oldest printed (by a publishing house) version of *The Nights* in Arabic by a non-European. It is primarily a reprinting of the ZER text.
- 1839–1842 — Calcutta II (4 volumes) is published. It claims to be based on an older Egyptian manuscript (which was never found). This version contains many elements and stories from the Habicht edition.
- 1838 — Torrens version in English.
- 1838–1840 — Edward William Lane publishes an English translation. Notable for its exclusion of content Lane found "immoral" and for its anthropological notes on Arab customs by Lane.
- 1882–1884 — John Payne publishes an English version translated entirely from Calcutta II, adding some tales from Calcutta I and Breslau.
- 1885–1888 — Sir Richard Francis Burton publishes an English translation from several sources (largely the same as Payne). His version accentuated the sexuality of the stories *vis-à-vis* Lane's bowdlerized translation.
- 1889–1904 — J. C. Mardrus publishes a French version using Bulaq and Calcutta II editions.
- 1984 — Muhsin Mahdi publishes an Arabic edition which he claims is faithful to the oldest Arabic versions surviving (primarily based on the Syrian manuscript in the Bibliothèque Nationale in combination with other early manuscripts of the Syrian branch).
- 1990s — Husain Haddawy publishes an English translation of Mahdi.

Literary themes and techniques

The *One Thousand and One Nights* and various tales within it make use of many innovative literary techniques, which the storytellers of the tales rely on for increased drama, suspense, or other emotions. Some of these date back to earlier Persian, Indian and Arabic literature, while others were original to the *One Thousand and One Nights*.

Frame story

An early example of the frame story, or framing device, is employed in the *One Thousand and One Nights*, in which the character Scheherazade narrates a set of tales (most often fairy tales) to the Sultan Shahriyar over many nights. Many of Scheherazade's tales are also frame stories, such as the *Tale of Sindbad the Seaman and Sindbad the Landsman* being a collection of adventures related by Sindbad the Seaman to Sindbad the Landsman. The concept of the frame story dates back to ancient Sanskrit literature, and was introduced into Persian and Arabic literature through the *Panchatantra*.

A girl with Parrot, scene from the One Thousand and One Nights

Story within a story

An early example of the "story within a story" technique can be found in the *One Thousand and One Nights*, which can be traced back to earlier Persian and Indian storytelling traditions, most notably the *Panchatantra* of ancient Sanskrit literature. The *Nights*, however, improved on the *Panchatantra* in several ways, particularly in the way a story is introduced. In the *Panchatantra*, stories are introduced as didactic analogies, with the frame story referring to these stories with variants of the phrase "If you're not careful, that which happened to the louse and the flea will happen to you." In the *Nights*, this didactic framework is the least common way of introducing the story, but instead a story is most commonly introduced through subtle means, particularly as an answer to questions raised in a previous tale.

An early example of the "story within a story within a story" device is also found in the *One Thousand and One Nights*, where the general story is narrated by an unknown narrator, and in this narration the stories are told by Scheherazade. In most of Scheherazade's narrations there are also stories narrated, and even in some of these, there are some other stories. This is particularly the case for the "Sinbad the Sailor" story narrated by Scheherazade in the *One Thousand and One Nights*. Within the "Sinbad the Sailor" story itself, the protagonist Sinbad the Sailor narrates the stories of his seven voyages to Sinbad the Porter. The device is also used to great effect in stories such as "The Three Apples" and "The Seven Viziers". In yet another tale Scheherazade narrates, "The Fisherman and the Jinni", the "Tale of the

Wazir and the Sage Duban" is narrated within it, and within that there are three more tales narrated.

Dramatic visualization

A Sufi Imam from the One Thousand and One Nights

Dramatic visualization is "the representing of an object or character with an abundance of descriptive detail, or the mimetic rendering of gestures and dialogue in such a way as to make a given scene 'visual' or imaginatively present to an audience". This technique dates back to the *One Thousand and One Nights*. An example of this is the tale of "The Three Apples" (see Crime fiction elements below).

Fate and destiny

A common theme in many *Arabian Nights* tales is fate and destiny. The Italian filmmaker Pier Paolo Pasolini observed:

> every tale in *The Thousand and One Nights* begins with an 'appearance of destiny' which manifests itself through an anomaly, and one anomaly always generates another. So a chain of anomalies is set up. And the more logical, tightly knit, essential this chain is, the more beautiful the tale. By 'beautiful' I mean vital, absorbing and exhilarating. The chain of anomalies always tends to lead back to normality. The end of every tale in *The One Thousand and One Nights* consists of a 'disappearance' of destiny, which sinks back to the somnolence of daily life ... The protagonist of the stories is in fact destiny itself.

Though invisible, fate may be considered a leading character in the *One Thousand and One Nights*. The plot devices often used to present this theme are coincidence, reverse causation and the self-fulfilling prophecy (see Foreshadowing below).

Foreshadowing

Early examples of the foreshadowing technique of repetitive designation, now known as "Chekhov's gun", occur in the *One Thousand and One Nights*, which contains "repeated references to some character or object which appears insignificant when first mentioned but which reappears later to intrude suddenly in the narrative". A notable example is in the tale of "The Three Apples" (see Crime fiction elements below).

Another early foreshadowing technique is *formal patterning*, "the organization of the events, actions and gestures which constitute a narrative and give shape to a story; when done well, formal patterning allows the audience the pleasure of discerning and anticipating the structure of the plot as it unfolds".

This technique also dates back to the *One Thousand and One Nights*.

Another form of foreshadowing is the self-fulfilling prophecy, which dates back to the story of Krishna in ancient Sanskrit literature. A variation of this device is the self-fulfilling dream, which dates back to medieval Arabic literature. Several tales in the *One Thousand and One Nights* use this device to foreshadow what is going to happen, as a special form of literary prolepsis. A notable example is "The Ruined Man who Became Rich Again through a Dream", in which a man is told in his dream to leave his native city of Baghdad and travel to Cairo, where he will discover the whereabouts of some hidden treasure. The man travels there and experiences misfortune, ending up in jail, where he tells his dream to a police officer. The officer mocks the idea of foreboding dreams and tells the protagonist that he himself had a dream about a house with a courtyard and fountain in Baghdad where treasure is buried under the fountain. The man recognizes the place as his own house and, after he is released from jail, he returns home and digs up the treasure. In other words, the foreboding dream not only predicted the future, but the dream was the cause of its prediction coming true. A variant of this story later appears in English folklore as the "Pedlar of Swaffham" and Paulo Coelho's "The Alchemist"; Jorge Luis Borges' collection of short stories *A Universal History of Infamy* featured his translation of this particular story into Spanish, as "The Story Of The Two Dreamers."

Another variation of the self-fulfilling prophecy can be seen in "The Tale of Attaf", where Harun al-Rashid consults his library (the House of Wisdom), reads a random book, "falls to laughing and weeping and dismisses the faithful *vizier*" Ja'far ibn Yahya from sight. Ja'afar, "disturbed and upset flees Baghdad and plunges into a series of adventures in Damascus, involving Attaf and the woman whom Attaf eventually marries." After returning to Baghdad, Ja'afar reads the same book that caused Harun to laugh and weep, and discovers that it describes his own adventures with Attaf. In other words, it was Harun's reading of the book that provoked the adventures described in the book to take place. This is an early example of reverse causation. Near the end of the tale, Attaf is given a death sentence for a crime he didn't commit but Harun, knowing the truth from what he has read in the book, prevents this and has Attaf released from prison. In the 12th century, this tale was translated into Latin by Petrus Alphonsi and included in his *Disciplina Clericalis*, alongside the "Sinbad the Sailor" story cycle. In the 14th century, a version of "The Tale of Attaf" also appears in the *Gesta Romanorum* and Giovanni Boccaccio's *The Decameron*.

Repetition

Leitwortstil is 'the purposeful repetition of words' in a given literary piece that "usually expresses a motif or theme important to the given story". This device occurs in the *One Thousand and One Nights*, which connects several tales together in a story cycle. The storytellers of the tales relied on this technique "to shape the constituent members of their story cycles into a coherent whole."

Thematic patterning is "the distribution of recurrent thematic concepts and moralistic motifs among the various incidents and frames of a story. In a skillfully crafted tale, thematic patterning may be arranged so as to emphasize the unifying argument or salient idea which disparate events and disparate frames have in common". This technique also dates back to the *One Thousand and One Nights* (and earlier).

Several different variants of the "Cinderella" story, which has its origins in the Egyptian story of Rhodopis, appear in the *One Thousand and One Nights*, including "The Second Shaykh's Story", "The Eldest Lady's Tale" and "Abdallah ibn Fadil and His Brothers", all dealing with the theme of a younger sibling harassed by two jealous elders. In some of these, the siblings are female, while in others they are male. One of the tales, "Judar and His Brethren", departs from the happy endings of previous variants and reworks the plot to give it a tragic ending instead, with the younger brother being poisoned by his elder brothers.

Satire and parody

The *Nights* contain many examples of sexual humour. Some of this borders on satire, as in the tale called "Ali with the Large Member" which pokes fun at obsession with human penis size.

Repetition is also used to humorous effect in the *One Thousand and One Nights*. Sheherezade sometimes follows up a relatively serious tale with a cruder or more broadly humorous version of the same tale. For example, "Wardan the Butcher's Adventure With the Lady and the Bear" is paralleled by "The King's Daughter and the Ape", "Harun al-Rashid and the Two Slave-Girls" by "Harun al-Rashid and the Three Slave-Girls", and "The Angel of Death With the Proud King and the Devout Man" by "The Angel of Death and the Rich King". The idea has been put forward that these pairs of tales are deliberately intended as examples of self parody, although this assumes a greater degree of editorial control by a single writer than the history of the collection as a whole would seem to indicate.

Unreliable narrator

The literary device of the unreliable narrator was used in several fictional medieval Arabic tales of the *One Thousand and One Nights*. In one tale, "The Seven Viziers" (also known as "Craft and Malice of Women or The Tale of the King, His Son, His Concubine and the Seven Wazirs"), a courtesan accuses a king's son of having assaulted her, when in reality she had failed to seduce him (inspired by the Qur'anic/Biblical story of Yusuf/Joseph). Seven viziers attempt to save his life by narrating seven stories to prove the unreliability of women, and the courtesan responds back by narrating a story to prove the unreliability of viziers. The unreliable narrator device is also used to generate suspense in "The Three Apples" and humor in "The Hunchback's Tale" (see Crime fiction elements below).

Crime fiction elements

The earliest known murder mystery and suspense thriller with multiple plot twists and detective fiction elements was "The Three Apples", also known as *Hikayat al-sabiyya 'l-muqtula* ("The Tale of the Murdered Young Woman"), one of the tales narrated by Scheherazade in the *One Thousand and One Nights*. In this tale, a fisherman discovers a heavy locked chest along the Tigris river and he sells it to the Abbasid Caliph, Harun al-Rashid, who then has the chest broken open only to find inside it the dead body of a young woman who was cut into pieces. Harun orders his vizier, Ja'far ibn Yahya, to solve the crime and find the murderer within three days or else he will have him executed instead. This whodunit mystery may thus be considered an archetype for detective fiction. Ja'far, however, fails to find the culprit before the deadline. Just when Harun is about to have Ja'far executed for his failure, a plot twist occurs when two men appear, one a handsome young man and the other an old man, both claiming to be the murderer. Both men argue and call each other liars as each attempts to claim responsibility for the murder. This continues until the young man proves that he is the murderer by accurately describing the chest in which the young woman was found.

The young man reveals that he was her husband and the old man her father, who was attempting to save his son-in-law by taking the blame. Harun then demands to know his motives for murdering his wife, and the young man then narrates his reasons as a flashback of events preceding Harun's discovery of the locked chest. He eulogizes her as a faultless wife and mother of his three children, and describes how she one day requested a rare apple when she was ill. He then describes his two-week long journey to Basra, where he finds three such apples at the Caliph's orchard. On his return to Baghdad, he finds out that she would no longer eat the apples because of her lingering illness. When he returns to work at his shop, he discovered a slave passing by with the same apple. He asked him about it and the slave replied that he received it from his girlfriend, who had three such apples that her husband found for her after a half-month journey. The young man then suspected his wife of unfaithfulness, rushed home, and demanded to know how many apples remained there. After finding one of the apples missing, he drew a knife and killed her. He then describes how he attempted to get rid of the evidence by cutting her body to pieces, wrapping it in multiple layers of shawls and carpets, hiding her body in a locked chest, and abandoning it in the Tigris river. Yet another twist occurs after he returns home and his son confesses to him that he had stolen one of the apples, and a slave had taken it and run off with it. The boy also confesses that he told the slave about his father's quest for the three apples. Out of guilt, the young man concludes his story by requesting Harun to execute him for his unjust murder. Harun, however, refuses to punish the young man out of sympathy, but instead sets Ja'far a new assignment: to find the tricky slave who caused the tragedy within three days, or be executed for his failure.

Ja'far yet again fails to find the culprit before the deadline has passed. On the day of the deadline, he is summoned to be executed for his failure. As he bids farewell to all his family members, he hugs his beloved youngest daughter last. It is then, by complete accident, that he discovers a round object in her pocket which she reveals to be an apple with the name of the Caliph written on it. In the story's twist ending, the girl reveals that she brought it from their slave, Rayhan. Ja'far thus realizes that his own slave was the culprit all along. He then finds Rayhan and solves the case as a result. Ja'far, however, pleads to Harun to forgive his slave and, in exchange, narrates to him the "Tale of Núr al-Dín Alí and His Son Badr al-Dín Hasan".

"The Three Apples" served as an inspiration for Hugo von Hofmannsthal's *The Golden Apple* (*Der Goldene Apfel*) (1897). It has also been noted that the flashback narrated by the young man in "The Three Apples" resembles the later story of Shakespeare's *Othello* (1603), which was itself based on "Un Capitano Moro", a tale from Giovanni Battista Giraldi's *Gli Hecatommithi* (1565).

Another *Nights* tale with crime fiction elements was "The Hunchback's Tale" story cycle which, unlike "The Three Apples", was more of a suspenseful comedy and courtroom drama rather than a murder mystery or detective fiction. The story is set in a fictional China and begins with a hunchback, the emperor's favourite comedian, being invited to dinner by a tailor couple. The hunchback accidentally chokes on his food from laughing too hard and the couple, fearful that the emperor will be furious, take his body to a Jewish doctor's clinic and leave him there. This leads to the next tale in the cycle, the "Tale of the Jewish Doctor", where the doctor accidentally trips over the hunchback's body, falls down the stairs with him, and finds him dead, leading him to believe that the fall had killed him. The doctor then dumps his body down a chimney, and this leads to yet another tale in the cycle, which continues with twelve tales in total, leading to all the people involved in this incident finding themselves in a courtroom, all making different claims over how the hunchback had died. Crime fiction elements are also present near the end of "The Tale of Attaf" (see Foreshadowing above).

Horror fiction elements

Haunting is used as a plot device in gothic fiction and horror fiction, as well as modern paranormal fiction. Legends about haunted houses have long appeared in literature. In particular, the *Arabian Nights* tale of "Ali the Cairene and the Haunted House in Baghdad" revolves around a house haunted by jinns. The *Nights* is almost certainly the earliest surviving literature that mentions ghouls, and many of the stories in that collection involve or reference ghouls. A prime example is the story *The History of Gherib and His Brother Agib* (from *Nights* vol. 6), in which Gherib, an outcast prince, fights off a family of ravenous Ghouls and then enslaves them and converts them to Islam.

Horror fiction elements are also found in "The City of Brass" tale, which revolves around a ghost town.

The horrific nature of Scheherazade's situation is magnified in Stephen King's *Misery*, in which the protagonist is forced to write a novel to keep his captor from torturing and killing him. The influence of the *Nights* on modern horror fiction is certainly discernible in the work of H. P. Lovecraft. As a child, he was fascinated by the adventures recounted in the book, and he attributes some of his creations to his love of the *1001 Nights*.

Science fiction elements

Several stories within the *One Thousand and One Nights* feature early science fiction elements. One example is "The Adventures of Bulukiya", where the protagonist Bulukiya's quest for the herb of immortality leads him to explore the seas, journey to Paradise and to Hell, and travel across the cosmos to different worlds much larger than his own world, anticipating elements of galactic science fiction;

along the way, he encounters societies of djinns, mermaids, talking serpents, talking trees, and other forms of life. In "Abu al-Husn and His Slave-Girl Tawaddud", the heroine Tawaddud gives an impromptu lecture on the mansions of the Moon, and the benevelont and sinister aspects of the planets.

In another *1001 Nights* tale, "Abdullah the Fisherman and Abdullah the Merman", the protagonist Abdullah the Fisherman gains the ability to breathe underwater and discovers an underwater submarine society that is portrayed as an inverted reflection of society on land, in that the underwater society follows a form of primitive communism where concepts like money and clothing do not exist. Other *Arabian Nights* tales also depict Amazon societies dominated by women, lost ancient technologies, advanced ancient civilizations that went astray, and catastrophes which overwhelmed them. "The City of Brass" features a group of travellers on an archaeological expedition across the Sahara to find an ancient lost city and attempt to recover a brass vessel that Solomon once used to trap a jinn, and, along the way, encounter a mummified queen, petrified inhabitants, life-like humanoid robots and automata, seductive marionettes dancing without strings, and a brass horseman robot who directs the party towards the ancient city, which has now become a ghost town. "The Ebony Horse" features a flying mechanical horse controlled using keys that could fly into outer space and towards the Sun. Some modern interpretations see this horse as a robot. The titular ebony horse can fly the distance of one year in a single day, and is used as a vehicle by the Prince of Persia, Qamar al-Aqmar, in his adventures across Persia, Arabia and Byzantium. This story appears to have influenced later European tales such as Adenes Le Roi's *Cleomades* and "The Squire's Prologue and Tale" told in Geoffrey Chaucer's *The Canterbury Tales*. "The City of Brass" and "The Ebony Horse" can be considered early examples of proto-science fiction. The "Third Qalandar's Tale" also features a robot in the form of an uncanny boatman.

The Nights in world culture

Literature

The influence of the versions of *The Nights* on world literature is immense. Writers as diverse as Henry Fielding to Naguib Mahfouz have alluded to the work by name in their own literature. Other writers who have been influenced by the *Nights* include John Barth, Jorge Luis Borges, Tom Holland, Salman Rushdie, Goethe, Walter Scott, Thackeray, Wilkie Collins, Elizabeth Gaskell, Nodier, Flaubert, Stendhal, Dumas, Gérard de Nerval, Gobineau, Pushkin, Tolstoy, Hofmannsthal, Conan Doyle, WB Yeats, HG Wells, Cavafy, Calvino, Georges Perec, HP Lovecraft, Marcel Proust, AS Byatt and Angela Carter.

This work has been influential in the West since it was translated in the 18th century, first by Antoine Galland. Many imitations were written, especially in France. Various characters from this epic have themselves become cultural icons in Western culture, such as Aladdin, Sinbad and Ali Baba. Part of its popularity may have sprung from the increasing historical and geographical knowledge, so that places of which little was known and so marvels were plausible had to be set further "long ago" or farther "far away"; this is a process that continues, and finally culminate in the fantasy world having little connection, if any, to actual times and places. Several elements from Arabian mythology and Persian mythology are now common in modern fantasy, such as genies, bahamuts, magic carpets, magic lamps, etc. When L. Frank Baum proposed writing a modern fairy tale that banished stereotypical elements, he included the genie as well as the dwarf and the fairy as stereotypes to go.

Examples of this influence include:

- Edgar Allan Poe wrote a "Thousand and Second Night" as a separate tale, called "The Thousand and Second Tale of Scheherazade". It depicts the 8th and final voyage of Sinbad the Sailor, along with the various mysteries Sinbad and his crew encounter; the anomalies are then described as footnotes to the story. While the king is uncertain—except in the case of the elephants carrying the world on the back of the turtle—that these mysteries are real, they are actual modern events that occurred in various places during, or before, Poe's lifetime. The story ends with the king in such disgust at the tale Scheherazade has just woven, that he has her executed the very next day. Caitlín R. Kiernan has written a story inspired by Poe's, titled "The Thousand and Third Tale of Scheherazade."
- Ramadan, an issue of Neil Gaiman's acclaimed comic book series The Sandman, draws on several of the stories of the Thousand and One Nights. In this tale, the Caliph Harun al-Rashid (who is a protagonist in many of the Nights) sells the "golden age of Baghdad" to the Prince of Stories, in order that it would never be forgotten. It is implied that the Thousand and One Nights is part of the result of that bargain.
- Bill Willingham, creator of the comic book series *Fables*, used the story of *The Nights* as the basis of his *Fables* prequel, *Fables: 1001 Nights of Snowfall*. In the book, Snow White tells the tales of the Fables, magical literary characters, to the sultan in order to avoid her impending death.
- Writer JinSeok Jeon and artist SeungHee Lee created an 11-volume comic series loosely based the original tale titled "One Thousand and One Nights", originally published in Korea and released in the U.S. by Yen Press. In this retelling, the character of Scheherazade is replaced by a male storyteller who is introduced to the sultan when he takes his sister's place in the sultan's harem.
- Two notable novels loosely based on *The Nights* are *Arabian Nights and Days* by Naguib Mahfouz and *When Dreams Travel* by Githa Hariharan. The children's novel *The Storyteller's Daughter* by Cameron Dokey is also loosely derived from *The Nights*.
- *The Nights* has also inspired poetry in English. Two examples are Alfred Tennyson's poem, "Recollections of the Arabian Nights" (1830) and William Wordsworth's "The Prelude" (1805).
- *The Book of One Thousand and One Nights* has an estranged cousin: *The Manuscript Found in Saragossa*, by Jan Potocki. A Polish noble of the late 18th century, he traveled the Orient looking for an original edition of *The Nights*, but never found it. Upon returning to Europe, he wrote his masterpiece, a multi-leveled frame tale. William Thomas Beckford's *Vathek*, one of the first gothic

novels, was also inspired by the *Nights*.

- The book is referenced in numerous works by Jorge Luis Borges.
- John Barth has alluded to *The Nights* or referenced it explicitly in many of his works, such as *The Last Voyage of Somebody the Sailor.* Scheherazade appears as a character in *The Tidewater Tales.* In addition, the "Dunyazadiad", one of a set of three novellas that make up Barth's fictional work Chimera (John Barth novel), is a re-telling of the Scheherazade framing story in which the author appears to Scheherazade from the future and recounts stories from the 1001 Nights to her in order to provide her with material with which to forestall her execution.
- In his criticism of mainstream cinema in "Metaphors on Vision", avant-garde filmmaker Stan Brakhage metaphorically compares Hollywood studio film making to Scheherazade's tales, calling it the, "... heroine of a thousand and one nights (Scheherazade must surely be the muse of this art)..."
- Craig Shaw Gardner wrote *Scheherazade's Night Out* in 1992.
- In 2005 playwright Jason Grote used the literary device of *One Thousand and One Arabian Nights* to create *1001*, combining the traditional Scheherazade story with literary and pop culture allusions ranging from Flaubert in Egypt, Jorge Luis Borges, Alfred Hitchcock's *Vertigo*, and Michael Jackson's *Thriller.* The main characters alternate between playing Scheherazade and Shahriyar and the Palestinian Dahna and the Jewish Alan, who are college students in love in modern New York. The play was premiered in Denver in 2006 and opened in New York City in October 2007 to strong reviews.
- In 2005 novelist Joseph Covino Jr adapted tales from the classical *1001 Nights* in two parts of an intended trilogy titled "Arabian Nights Lost: Celestial Verses I&II."
- The *Nights* also had an influence on modern Japanese literature. George Fyler Townsend's revised edition of the *Arabian Nights* was the first European literary work to be translated into the Japanese language during the Meiji era, by Nagamine Hideki in 1875. The Japanese translation was entitled *Arabiya Monogatari* ("Arabian Stories" or literally "Stormy Night Stories"), as part of the monogatari genre. Though the book was intriguing to Japanese readers who then had very little knowledge of Arabic culture or the Middle East in general, the *Nights* didn't gain popularity in Japan until a more Japanified translation, entitled *Zensekai Ichidai Kisho* (*The Most Curious Book in the Whole World*), was produced by Inoue Tsutomu in 1888. His translation exerted a great influence on the literature of the Meiji, Taishō and Shōwa periods, with writers and poets such as Hinatsu Kōnosuke, Hakushū Kitahara and Mokutaro Kinoshita citing the work as an influence on their own works. In the early 20th century, other translations from the Lane and Burton editions were also published, including ones from the Lane edition by Kōnosuke and Morita Sōhei, as well a translation of the Andrew Lang edition by Daisui Sugitani, and translations of individual tales by Iwaya Sazanami.
- David Foster's 2009 novel *Sons of the Rumour* is a pastiche of the *Nights*.

Film, television and radio

There have been many adaptations of *The Nights* for television, cinema and radio.

The atmosphere of *The Nights* influenced such films as Fritz Lang's 1921 *Der müde Tod*, the 1924 Hollywood film *The Thief of Baghdad* starring Douglas Fairbanks, and its 1940 British remake. Several stories served as source material for *The Adventures of Prince Achmed* (1926), the oldest surviving feature-length animated film.

In the late 1930s, Fleischer Studios made three two-reel animated *Popeye* cartoons in color for Paramount Pictures. All three cartoons, known also as the *Popeye Color Specials* (or *Features*), were adapted from *The Nights*: *Popeye the Sailor Meets Sindbad the Sailor*, *Popeye the Sailor Meets Ali Baba's Forty Thieves*, and *Aladdin and His Wonderful Lamp*.

One of Hollywood's first feature films to be based on *The Nights* was in 1942, with the movie called *Arabian Nights*. It starred Maria Montez as Scheherazade, Sabu Dastagir as Ali Ben Ali and Jon Hall as Harun al-Rashid. The storyline bears virtually no resemblance to the traditional version of the book. In the film, Scheherazade is a dancer who attempts to overthrow Caliph Harun al-Rashid and marry his brother. After Scheherazade's initial coup attempt fails and she is sold into slavery, many adventures then ensue. Maria Montez and Jon Hall also starred in the 1944 film *Ali Baba and the Forty Thieves*.

In the 1952 Universal Pictures movie *The Golden Blade*, Harun Al-Rashid (Rock Hudson) uses a magical sword that makes him invincible to free Baghdad from the evil vizier Jafar and his son Hadi and win the love of the beautiful princess Khairuzan (Piper Laurie).

Perhaps the most famous Sinbad film was the 1958 movie *The Seventh Voyage of Sinbad*, produced by the stop-motion animation pioneer Ray Harryhausen. Harryhausen also provided the stop-motion effects for *The Golden Voyage of Sinbad* (1974) and *Sinbad and the Eye of the Tiger* (1977).

In 1959 UPA released an animated feature about Mr. Magoo, based on *1001 Arabian Nights*.

Osamu Tezuka worked on two (very loose) feature film adaptations, the children's film *Sinbad no Bōken* in 1962 and then *Senya Ichiya Monogatari* in 1969, an adult-oriented animated feature film.

The most commercially successful movie based on *The Nights* was *Aladdin*, the 1992 animated movie by the Walt Disney Company, which starred the voices of Scott Weinger and Robin Williams. The film led to several sequels and a television series of the same name.

"The Voyages of Sinbad" has been adapted for television and film several times, most recently in the 2003 animated feature *Sinbad: Legend of the Seven Seas*, featuring the voices of Brad Pitt and Catherine Zeta-Jones.

A recent well-received television adaptation was the Emmy Award-winning miniseries *Arabian Nights*, directed by Steve Barron and starring Mili Avital as Scheherazade and Dougray Scott as Shahryar. It was originally shown over two nights on April 30, and May 1, 2000 on ABC in the United States and BBC One in the United Kingdom.

In 2001, the *Radio Tales* series produced a trilogy of dramas adapted from the Arabian Nights, including the stories of Aladdin, Ali Baba, and Sindbad.

Other notable versions of *The Nights* include the famous 1974 Italian movie *Il fiore delle mille e una notte* by Pier Paolo Pasolini and the 1990 lFrench movie *Les 1001 nuits*, in which Catherine Zeta-Jones made her debut playing Scheherazade. There are also numerous Bollywood movies inspired by the book, including *Aladdin and Sinbad*. In this version the two heroes meet and share in each other's adventures; the djinn of the lamp is female, and Aladdin marries her rather than the princess.

In 2009, the BBC Radio 7 science fiction series *Planet B* featured an episode set in a virtual world which had merged *The Nights* with a wargame.

Alif Laila (Thousand Nights) is a TV series based on the stories from The Arabian Nights. It was produced by Sagar Films (Pvt. Ltd.) and has been presented on air so far on DD National, India, SAB TV, India and ARY Digital, Pakistan.

Music

- In 1888, Russian composer Nikolai Rimsky-Korsakov completed his Op. 35 *Scheherazade*, in four movements, based upon four of the tales from *The Nights*: "The Sea and Sinbad's Ship", "The Kalendar Prince", "The Young Prince and The Young Princess", and "Festival at Baghdad."
- There have been several *Arabian Nights* musicals and operettas, either based on particular tales or drawing on the general atmosphere of the book. Most notable are *Chu Chin Chow* (1916) and *Kismet* (1953), not to mention several musicals and innumerable pantomimes on the story of "Aladdin."
- 1990 saw the premiere of *La Noche de las Noches*, a work for string quartet and electronics by Ezequiel Viñao (based on a reading from Burton's "Book of the Thousand Nights and a Night")
- In 1975, the band Renaissance released an album called *Scheherazade and Other Stories*. The second half of this album consists entirely of the "Song of Scheherazade", an orchestral-rock composition based on *The Nights*.
- In the song "Sheherazade", on his 1988 album *One More Story*, Peter Cetera refers to the *One Thousand and One Nights* tale.
- In 1999, power metal band Kamelot included a song on their album *The Fourth Legacy* called "Nights of Arabia".
- The song "One Thousand and One Nights" by J-Pop band See-Saw, used as the opening theme song for the second part of the four-part OVA .hack//Liminality ("In the Case of Yuki Aihara"), references *The Nights* in both the title and the lyrics.
- In 2003, Nordic experimental indie pop group When released an album called *Pearl Harvest* with lyrics from *The Nights*.

- In 2004, psychedelic trance group 1200 Micrograms released song called *1001 Arabian Nights* on *The Time Machine* album.
- In 2007, Japanese pop duo BENNIE K released a single titled "1001 Nights", also releasing a music video strongly based on *The Nights*.
- In 2007, the Finnish Symphonic metal band Nightwish wrote a song "Sahara" on their album *Dark Passion Play* which relates to the *1001 Nights* stories.
- 2008 saw the birth of Australian metalcore band, Ebony Horse, named after the tale "The Ebony Horse."
- The Dutch music group "CH!PZ" has also released a song called *1001 Arabian Nights* and also has a film clip to go along with it which illustrates one of the stories.
- There is a tourist attraction by the name of Arabian Nights in Orlando, Florida, which is based on the One Thousand and One Nights storyline and features a Princess Scheherazade as the central character in a musical dinner show.

See also: List of stories within The Book of One Thousand and One Nights

Games

- The first expansion set for *Magic: The Gathering* was "Arabian Nights", containing cards based on and inspired by *One Thousand and One Nights*. This included a card called "Shahrazad" which required the two players to play a separate game within the current game."Players play a MAGIC subgame, using their libraries as their decks. Each player who doesn't win the subgame loses half his or her life, rounded up."-http://gatherer.wizards.com/Pages/Card/Details.aspx?multiverseid=980
- Jordan Mechner stated that *The Nights* was an inspiration for his popular *Prince of Persia* series.
- *Tales of the Arabian Nights* is a paragraph-based story-telling board game first produced by West End Games in 1985. A second edition was published by Edition Erlkönig in 1999, and a third edition by Z-Man Games is due out in July 2009.
- *The Magic of Scheherazade*, a 1989 game produced by the Japanese company Culture Brain for the Nintendo Entertainment System, takes its title from the female protagonist of the Arabian Nights and includes many of the typical trappings of Arabian Nights tales, but has little, if any, direct connection to the tales.
- The setting of the 1990 EGA PC adventure game *Quest for Glory II: Trial by Fire* is based on *The Nights*.
- In 1994 Krisalis developed an Amiga platform game called Arabian Nights with the main character being Sinbad aiming to rescue the princess.

- *The Nights* is the basis for the story of the video game *Sonic and the Secret Rings*. In the story, Sonic the Hedgehog is pulled in to the story by Shahra The Ring Genie in order to save the Arabian Nights which is being erased by the main villain Erazor Djinn. Other recurring Sonic characters turn up as characters from the Nights, such as Tails as Ali Baba, Knuckles as Sinbad, and Doctor Eggman as King Shahryār.
- *One Thousand and One Nights*, a storytelling game by Meguey Baker, puts the players in the roles of courtiers in the Sultan's palace who are forbidden to leave for various reasons. To pass the time, they take turns telling stories and casting each other as various characters in the tales as they attempt to earn enough favor in the court to win their freedom.
- *One Thousand and One Nights* is the name of a Tomahawk weapon available for the character Lexaeus in the video game Kingdom Hearts 358/2 Days.

See also

- List of stories from *The Book of One Thousand and One Nights* (according to the Richard Francis Burton translation).
- List of characters from *The Book of One Thousand and One Nights*
- Scheherazade in popular culture
- *Chimera*, the 1972 National Book Award-winning novel by John Barth, which includes a novella re-imagining the story of Scheherazade and her sister, Dunyazade.
- Arabic literature
- Persian literature

One Thousand and One Nights as a book.

Further reading

- *In Arabian Nights: A search of Morocco through its stories and storytellers* by Tahir Shah, Doubleday, 2008. This is a book that explores the ancient living tradition of storytelling that bridges East and West, yet somehow seems to survive at much more pervasively vibrant levels in contemporary Moroccan culture. [1]

External links

- Takhir Sabirov [2]
- Interview with Claudia Ott: A New Chapter in the History of Arab Literature [3]
- 1001 Nights [4]
- Journal of the 1001 Nights [5] – An online blog resource for new and developing news, scholarship and info on the 1001 (aka The Arabian) Nights and their many manifestations.
- Craft and Malice of Women, or The Tale of the King, His Son, His Concubine and the Seven Wazirs [6]

References

- Yamanaka, Yuriko and Nishio, Tetsuo (ed.) *The Arabian Nights and Orientalism – perspectives from East and West London*, London: I.B.Tauris, 2006. ISBN 1-85043-768-8
- Encyclopedia Iranica, "ALF LAYLA WA LAYLA (One thousand nights and one night) Ch. Pellat [7]
- Encyclopedia Iranica, "HAZARAFSANA"(A Thousand Stories) [8]
- *The Thousand Nights and a Night* in several classic translations [9], including unexpurgated version by Sir Richard Francis Burton, and John Payne translation, with additional material.
- *Stories From One Thousand and One Nights*, (Lane and Poole translation): Project Bartleby edition [10]
- *The Arabian Nights* [11] (includes illustrated Lang and (expurgated) Burton translations), presented by the Electronic Literature Foundation [12]
- Jonathan Scott translation of Arabian Nights [13]
- Notes on the influences and context of the *Thousand and One Nights* [14]
- (expurgated) Sir Richard Burton's 1885 translation, annotated for English study. [15]
- *The Arabian Nights by Andrew Lang* [16] at Project Gutenberg
- "The Thousand-And-Second Tale of Scheherazade" by Edgar Allan Poe (Wikisource)
- Arabian Nights [17] Six full-color plates of illustrations from the 1001 Nights which are in the public domain

Film and television links

- Takhir Sabirov [2]
- Arabian Nights (1942) [18] IMDb
- Il Fiore delle mille e una notte (1974) [19] IMDb
- Sinbad: Legend of the Seven Seas [20] Official website

Book links

- Librivox audiobook of Lang's *The Arabian Night's Entertainments* [21]
- [22] French edition (tr. Galland, 1822)
- Arabian Nights by Andrew Lang [23] – ereader formatted book from feedbooks
- Translation on Bosnian language by Prof. Dr. Esad Duraković, *1001 noć 1-4*—, komplet (4 books), Groups: Pripovijetke, ISBN 9958-22-054-7, Publisher: Ljiljan, 1999 (overview [24]) [25]
- Saj from The One Thousand and One Nights [26]
- Arabian Nights Richard F. Burton [27] – Near exact reprint of Burton Club 1903 edition. Paperback 16 Volume including Supplemental Tales

pnb:الف لیل

Hamzanama

Hamzanama

The **Hamzanama** (Persian: حمزه نامه, Epic of Hamza) or **Dastan-e-Amir Hamza** (Persian: داستان امیر حمزه, Adventures of Amir Hamza) narrates the legendary exploits of Amir Hamza, the uncle of the prophet of Islam. An illustrated manuscript of the *Hamzanama* was created about 1558–1573 under the Mughal emperor Akbar. As a book, the *Hamzanama* was designed to augment the story, as traditionally told in dastan performances. This romance originated more than 1,000 years ago, probably in Persia, and subsequently spread throughout the Islamic world in oral and written forms.

This large-scale painting depicts the Battle of Mazandaran. It is number 38 in the 7th volume of the *Hamzanama*, as inscribed between the legs of the man in the bottom center. It depicts a battle scene in which the protagonists Khwajah 'Umar and Hamzah and their armies engage in fierce battle. Originally, the faces were depicted; these were subsequently erased by iconoclasts, and repainted in more recent times.

Manuscripts of the *Hamzanama*

The illustrated manuscript created during the Akbar's reign originally comprised 1,400 canvas folios. On one side of most of the folios is a painting, about 54 cm x 69 cm in area, done in a fusion of Persian and Indian styles. On the other side of most of the folios is Persian text in Nasta'liq script. The folios are ordered, and the text on the back of one folio accompanies the painting on the subsequent folio. The bulk of these folios are to be found in the Victoria and Albert Museum and the British Museum in London. Further the Austrian Museum of Applied Art (MAK) in Vienna possesses another bulk of these folios and organized in 2009 the exhibition *GLOBAL:LAB, Art as a Message. Asia and Europe 1500-1700*, which showed the whole collection of the *Hamzanama* of the museum.

The colophon of this manuscript is still missing. None of the folios of this manuscript so far found is signed. According to Badauni and Shahnawaz Khan the work of preparing the illustrations was supervised initially by Mir Sayyid Ali and subsequently by Abdus Samad. It took fifteen years to complete the work.

The *Dastan-e-Amir Hamza* existed in several manuscript versions. One version by Navab Mirza Aman Ali Khan Ghalib Lakhnavi was printed in 1855 and published by the Hakim Sahib Press, Calcutta, India. This version was later embellished by Abdullah Bilgrami and published from the Naval Kishore Press, Lucknow, in 1871.

References

- Farooqi, Musharraf Ali (2007), *The Adventures of Amir Hamza* (New York: Random House Modern Library)
- Seyller, John (2002), *The Adventures of Hamza, Painting and Storytelling in Mughal India*, Freer Gallery of Art and Arthur M. Sackler Gallery, Smithsonian Institution, Washington, DC, in association with Azimuth Editions Limited, London, ISBN 1-898592-23-3 (Contains the most complete set of reproductions of Hamzanama paintings and text translations.)

External links

- *The Adventures of Amir Hamza* - the first complete and unabridged translation of the Dastan-e Amir Hamza [1]
- Online exhibit of *The Adventures of Hamza* at the Smithsonian Institution [2]
- *A Masterpiece of Sensuous Communication: The Hamzanama of Akbar* [3] (images in pdf file [4], Section II)
- Hamzanama at the [[Victoria & Albert Museum [5]], London]

Lake Saiful Muluk

Lake Saiful Muluk

Saiful Muluk	
in spring	
Location	Kaghan Valley
Coordinates	34°52′37″N 73°41′40″E
Basin countries	Pakistan
Surface area	2.75km
Surface elevation	3,224 m (10,578 ft)

Lake Saiful Muluk (Urdu: سیف الملوک) is a lake located at the northern end of the Kaghan Valley (34°52′37.34″N 73°41′37.71″E) near Naran. It is in the north east of Mansehra District in the Khyber-Pakhtunkhwa province, Pakistan. At an altitude of 3,224 m (10,578 feet) above sea level it is amongst one of the highest lakes in Pakistan.

Lake Saiful-muluk near Naran during the month of June

The lake is accessible by a 14 km road from Naran (which is accessible by a road from

Mansehra via Balakot and Kaghan) during the summer months. On foot, the trek from Naran to the lake takes about 1-2 hours. The water is clear with a slight green tone. The clarity of the water comes from the multiple glaciers all around the high basin which feed the lake.

Newly developed bridge at Lake Saifal Malook

The weather here is moderate during day time while the temperature drops to minus degrees at night.

A fairy tale called *Saiful Muluk*, written by the famous sufi poet Mian Muhammad Bakhsh, is associated with the lake. It is the story of prince of Persia who fell in love with a fairy princess at the lake. The impact of the lake beauty is of such extent that people believe that fairies come down to lake in full moon.

A poet and writer from Balakot, Ahmad Hussain Mujahid, has written the story of Saif ul Malook. The first edition of the book Saif ul Malook was published in 1999.

Tourism

The Guardian ranked Lake Saiful Muluk as the 5th Best Tourist Destination in Pakistan. Mansehra District has had a flourishing tourism industry in the past due to its many mountain ranges and the Saiful Muluk Lake, however since the 2005 earthquake the region has seen a decrease in tourists. This lake is about three thousand feet above the ground level of Naran, this beautiful lake reflects many colors in minutes. Lately there has been an interest in building hotels in the area.

See also

- Lulusar lake
- Ansoo Lake
- Dudipatsar lake

External links

- PTDC Official website [1]
- Picture Tour of Saif ul Muluk [2]
- Jheel Saif ul muluk in Naran Valley [3]

pnb:سیف الملوک

Churel

Churel

A **churel**, also written as "churail", or rather "chudail" (pronounced chew-dail) (Devanagari: चुडेल) is a female ghost out of Hindu folklore. She appears either as a hideous creature with long sagging breasts and unkempt hair, or as a beautiful young woman who can charm any man. Often, her feet are backward, and she has an unnaturally long and thick black tongue. The churel is said to be the unhappy ghost of a woman who died in childbirth or while menstruating. This connection means that she sucks blood, a habit shared with another monster, the vampire, and because young men are the cause of her death, the Churel always drinks from young men, beginning with the one she loved in life. The churel usually lives near small rivers or springs. She is either seen wearing a white or a red sari, representing a widow or a bride respectively. Along with this there's also a group of people telling that a churel is a spirit with enormous power who has sacrificed herself by giving her back part of meat in some ceremony of getting powers through black magic and that they can not be sometimes be found at the place of their death too.

Pakistani folklore

Pakistani folklore

Pakistan has a wide variety of folklore, mostly circulated regionally. However, certain tales have related variants in other regions of the country or in neighbouring countries. Some folktales like Shirin and Farhad are told in Pakistan, Iran, Afghanistan, Turkey, and almost all nations of Central Asia and Middle East, with all having claimed the folklore to have originated in their land. *Pakistani mythology* here means the myths and sacred narratives of the culturally and linguistically related group of ancient peoples who inhabited the ancient Pakistan and its borderlands.

A page from *Kelileh va Demneh* (dated 1429, from Herat, a Persian translation of the *Panchatantra*) depicts the manipulative jackal-vizier, Dimna, trying to lead his lion-king into war.

Provincial folklore

The provinces of Pakistan are known by the love stories in their folklore that have been immortalized by singers, reciters and storytellers of the regions.

A depiction of Nasreddin

Baloch folklore

Balochi folklore is alive with the love stories of Hani and Shah Murad Chakar, Shahdad and Mahnaz, Lallah and Granaz, Bebarg and Granaz, and Mast and Sammo, among others. The war tales of the Baloch are equally stirring. The *chap*, a Baloch style of dancing, has a curious rhythm distinguished by an inertial back sway with every forward step. Baloch music has a unique flavour of its own.

Kashmiri folklore

Kashmiri regions in the north are equally rich in folklore.

Pakhtun folklore

In the Pukhtun areas of the northwest, the North-West Frontier Province is the home of energetic warlike dancers, the most prominent being the Khattak dance, which bears the name of the tribe that dances it. The romantic tale of Adam Khan and Durkhanai features a lute player (*rabab*) whose music earns the love of a beautiful girl, although she hasn't seen him yet.

Punjabi folklore

Main article: Punjabi folklore

Many folk tales from Punjab have been disseminated worldwide by the Punjabi diaspora, especially in the UK and USA. The tale of two lovers, Heer and Ranjha, is based in the Pakistani part of the Punjab, in a city called Jhang. Today it is celebrated in songs, movies, theatre, and quotations. One may call a romantic person a Ranjha, meaning he is a devoted lover. Similarly a girl in love may be called "Heer." Apart from the epic of Hir and Ranjha, the Punjab has a rich tradition of ballads, folk tales, folk music and dance. The folklore of the Potohar Plateau of the north shows a local variant, while the lush green irrigated agriculture of the central plains is home to more sophisticated forms of folklore. The oldest living urban centre of Multan in the south is home to gentler forms of music and dance.

Saraiki folklore

Saraiki areas in the south are equally rich in folklore.

Sindhi folklore

Sindh in the south is equally rich in folklore. The love story of Sassi, who pines for her lover Punnu, is known and sung in every Sindhi settlement. Other examples of the folklore of Sindh include the stories of Umer Marvi and Suhuni Mehar.

Cultural folklore

The Muslim high culture of Pakistan and rest of South Asia emphasizes Arabic, Persian and Turkish culture. Islamic mythology and Persian mythology is part of Pakistani folklore, as Islamic religion and Persian culture dominate Pakistan. The Shahnameh, *One Thousand and One Nights* and *Sinbad the Sailor* were part of the education of Muslim children in Pakistan before English education was imposed by the British colonialism.

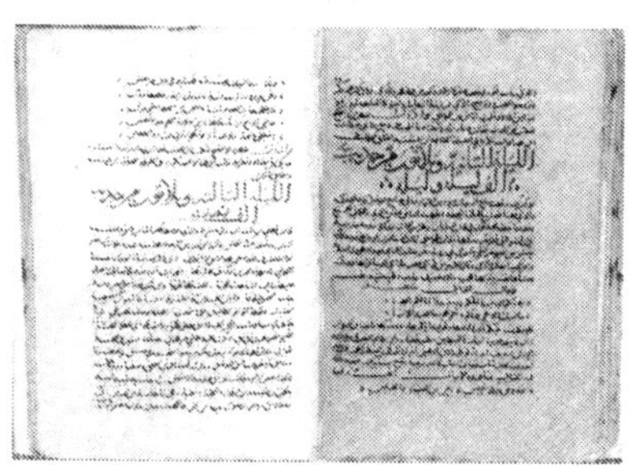

Arabic manuscript of *One Thousand and One Nights* dating back to the 1300s

See also

- Adam Khan and Durkhanai
- Arabian mythology
- Gulistan of Sa'di
- Hani and Sheh Mureed
- Hatim al-Tai
- Heer Ranjha
- Islamic mythology
- Layla and Majnun
- LiLa Chanesar
- Magic carpet
- Mirza Sahiba
- Momal Rano
- Mullah Nasreddin
- Noori Jam Tamachi
- One Thousand and One Nights
- Paristan
- Peri

- Persian mythology
- Prince Saiful Malook and Badri Jamala
- Punjabi Kisse
- Rostam and Sohrab
- Rostam
- Sassi Punnun
- Shah Jo Risalo
- Shahnameh
- Shirin and Farhad
- Sinbad the Sailor
- Sohni Mahiwal
- The Tale of the Four Dervishes
- Turkish folklore
- Yusuf and Zulaikha
- Yusuf Khan and Sherbano

Ayyār

Ayyār

Áyyār, (Persian: عيار, Arabic plural is 'ayyarun, Persian plural is 'ayyaran') refers to a person associated with a class of warriors in Iraq and Iran from the 9th to the 12th centuries. The word literally means *vagabond*. Ayyars were associated with futuwwa, or medieval Islamic organizations located in cities.

Emergence

'Ayyarun fought for Islam in Asia, though most of the writing about them centers on their Baghdad activities of the 10th to the 12th centuries. Baghdad was ruled by the Buyids (945–1055), and was a very lawless city, caused by fighting between Sunnis and Shi'ites. They did many terrible things such as extorting taxes on roads and markets, burning wealthy quarters and markets, and looting the homes of the rich by night. For several years (1028–33), Al-Burjumi and Ibn al-Mawsili, leaders of the 'ayyarun, ruled the city due to governmental instability.

Reputation

The 'ayyarun have been commonly called thieves and robbers, though these activities are highlighted during times of weak government and civil war, when their role as a military force most likely made them fight on multiple sides, angering many. During times of more stable government, their unlawful activities decreased, and when the Seljuqs ruled in the 12th century, their activities almost ceased. The 'ayyarun also made war against much of society in reaction to social injustices.

Regional influence

Outside of Baghdad, the 'ayyarun were closely allied with the middle class, and helped maintain the current order. The Saffarids (861-1003) of eastern Iran were in fact an 'ayyarun dynasty. They are thought by some historians to have contributed to the weakening of Baghdad, clearing the way for the horrific destruction of the city by the Mongols.

References

- AYYĀR [1], Encyclopedia Iranica

External links

- Library reference [2]
- Word definition [3]
- Primary Source reference [4]
- Newspaper article [5]

Adam Khan and Durkhanai

Adam Khan and Durkhanai

Adam Khan Aw Durkhanai is a classic Pashtun romance which has been called the Pashto Romeo and Juliet along with Yusuf Khan and Sherbano. It is considered classic pashto literature.

External links

- Adam Khan Durkhanai [1]

Yusuf Khan and Sherbano

Yusuf Khan and Sherbano

Along with Adam Khan and Durkhanai, **Yusuf Khan and Sherbano** is considered a famous Pashtun folktale on par with Romeo and Juliet.

Story

The story, written by the pashtun poet from Ismaila Ali Haider Joshi, goes as follows:

Yusuf Khan of Ismaila(Torayghunday), (a village in Swabi), was a hunter. That this passion for the chase be satisfied, he walked daily from his village to the nearby massif of the Kharamar hill. Towering a full five hundred meters above the fertile Yusufzai plains, Kharamar in those days was thickly covered with pine, acacia and wild olive and in the ravine, deer and partridge were populous. He would always take his father's hunting dogs with him and bring back a bag full of game.

Between his home and Kharamar lay the village of the fair Sher Bano. And so it was only a matter of time that the two saw each other. Cupid's arrows flew and the two hearts were kindled with the warmth of love. Now, much ink has been spilled on the subject of the cousin (Tarboor) among the Pakhtuns, its convoluted jealousies and intrigues and how its venom only increases in the event of one's father's death. And since Yusuf Khan's father had long been dead, his cousins now ganged up to deny him not only his father's legacy, but his beloved one as well.

The intrigues that followed forced young Yusuf Khan to abandon his homeland, his aged mother and young sister to seek employment in distant india which was then ruled by the Muslim Mughals. There our hero found service in the army of the King Akbar. Time flew and Yusuf Khan rose in standing until he was assigned command of a body of troops. If that was to uplift his spirits, depressing news arrived from distant home under the dark loom of Kharamar: despite the resistance by his mother, sister and Sher Bano herself, his cousins had contrived Sher Bano's betrothal with another man.

Taking leave from the court Yusuf Khan rode out westward at the head of his contingent of Mughal soldiers. As luck would have it, he arrived on the day his Sher Bano was being forcibly wedded.

Yusuf Khan rode rough-shod into the celebrations, disrupting everything and slaying some of the vilest of his cousins. Those of his cousins that survived, overawed by the power given him by imperial service, made peace with him - or at least pretended to do so.

Yusuf Khan then wedded his lady and together they began a new and happy life. One day, not long afterwards, as Yusuf Khan returned home after a day in the field, Sher Bano was disappointed to see he had brought home no game to be cooked. She spoke her sentiment and Yusuf Khan set out for Kharamar with two of his cousins who now pretended to be his friends. Upon the mountain they shot a deer that fell down a gully.

As he was lowering himself down the gorge, Yusuf Khan's cousins, forever looking to avenge their brothers' death, cut the rope. Our hero fell to his death. Upon hearing of the end of her man, Sher Bano came up the mountain and there committed suicide.

Other media

Main article: Yousuf Khan Sher Bano

There was a film remake. The Pashtun poet, the late Ali Haider Joshi, was the only Pushto poet who composed the famous folk story "Yousaf Khan Sher Bano" while producing the first-ever Pushto movie, which is still very popular in the Pakhtun community. This movie was mostly filmed in Karamar Mountain (Yousaf Khan and Sher Bano lie buried on its peak) and other areas of the district where the real story occurred. "The verification of Yousaf Khan and Sher Bano's love story became the cornerstone of his poetic career. "The credit of popularity of this wonderful Pushto folk story also goes to Joshi," said Dr Raj Wali Shah Khattak, the director of Pushto Academy, University of Peshawar in 2004.

See also

- Adam Khan And Durkhanai
- Heer Ranjha
- Noori Jam Tamachi

External links

- Pukhtun Women [1]

Prince Saiful Malook and Badri Jamala

Prince Saiful Malook and Badri Jamala

Prince Saiful Mulook and Badi-ul- Jamal is a classic fable in the Hazara region of modern day Pakistan. It tells the story of a Prince's love for a fairy; the name Saiful Malook refers to a lake in northern Pakistan.

Poetry

There is also a famous poem about the story written by famous poet Mian Muhammad Baksh who wrote the classic story into poetic verse. The poem entitled **Saif-Ul-Mulook** is written in the Potohari / Hindko language and very much popular in the Potohar, Kashmir, [[Hazara, Pakistan|Hazarah]] regions of Northern Pakistan.

The story of Saif ul Muluk is that the Prophet Joseph (yosuf) is asked who will be the handsomest man after him and he has two seals made, and says that the man will be my descendant and will inherit these seals, and so after many years when Saif ul Muluk comes of age and is bequeathed these seals among many other treasures, on one of them is a picture of himself and on the other is a picture of the beautiful fairy Princess Badi-ul-Jamal, meaning the glory of the moon, he falls in love and thus begins his long arduous journey to find her. Later when he does find her, he learns that her soul is trapped in the tallest mountain of the lake which is now called "Saif ul Muluk" and the mountain is "Malka Purbat" which means "the Mountain of the Fairies" and that she is bound to Jinn, and he can only free her when the Jinn is dead, but he cannot defeat him using ordinary means, for the Jinn has hidden his soul in talisman of some sort and hidden it away, Saiful Maluk and his army succeed in finding the talisman and killing the jinn but igniting a 40 year war between the jinn of the earth and those who dwell in the spirit world.

The Land of the fairies,no doubt it earned its name just for nothing,as they say seeing is believing. The breath taking view of the lake and the towering "malka parbat"meaning the Queen Mountain standing tall and invincible presents a classical picture of His art. "Thou art everywhere, I see thee in here". Love on first sight made me say this and I was awe-struck at its majesty and grandeaur. The legend of the lake is very interesting and romantic. A Prince, Saif ul Malook fell in love with a fairy princess, Badr u Jamal, whom he saw in his dreams. The prince was restless until a Darvaish (holy man) told him where to find her (i.e. by the lake) and that he had to go through a tough exam to be able to marry the fairy because the prince was a human and she was a fairy. Thus the prince marched on his quest for the impossible in the name of love. He waited by the lake where there was no habitation, (there still isn't), no food, nothing. His long wait of 12 years, finally reaped harvest and one good morning he saw the fairy come to bathe with her maids and friends in the lake. The prince hid her wings as advised by the holy man. The fairy was very tense at not finding her wings. Eventually the prince appeared and told her about his tale of love and long wait, which moved the fairy and they agreed to marry. But there is always a villain. So a Deuo Safaid (the white giant) who was himself in love with the fairy got jealous and furious. In rage the giant cried and thus tear lake (ansoo jheel, approx. 2 miles away) was formed. The giant stepped angrily, the dam broke and the outlet to the lake Saif-ul-Mulook was formed. The prince and the fairy princess fled away in a cave (which still exists and its length is unknown to this day). The legend says that both the prince and the fairy live in the centre of the lake saifulmulook, and on every full moon night they emerge mounted on a white flying horse, the pagasus, from the centre of the lake. The depth of the lake has not been measured to this day,the last effort they say was made in late 90s but the measuring chain weighing 5 tons went down and vanished and the mystery of the lake dares us!catch me if u can.

Noori Jam Tamachi

Noori Jam Tamachi

Noori Jam Tamachi (Sindhi: نوري □ام تماچي) is a mythical Sindhi folk tale which happened in the region of Sindh, Pakistan. It is a tragic love story, similar to Romeo and Juliet, between King Jam Tamachi, belonging to Unar tribe, Noori, belonging to community of fishermen (Muhanas).

According to the legend, Noori was buried in the Kalri Lake. Today there is a mausoleum in the middle of the lake for Noori that is visited by hundreds of devotees daily.

The legend has been retold countless times, and is often presented as metaphor for divine love by Sufis. One of its most famous renderings is in Sindhi poetry by Shah Abdul Latif Bhita'i in his Shah Jo Risalo. The legend of Noori Jam Tamachi took place around the Kalri Lake in Pakistan, and to this day there is a shrine in the middle of the lake marking Noor's grave. Everyday hundreds of devotees visit the shrine.

See also

- Jam Tamachi
- Heer Ranjha
- Momal Rano
- Umar Marvi
- LiLa Chanesar
- Sohni Mahiwal
- Sassi Punnun
- Sindhi literature
- Shah Abdul Latif Bhittai

External links

- Legend of Nuri Jam Tamachi [1]
- Shah Jo Risalo - The Selection, translated by: Elsa Kazi in English Language [2]

The Tale of the Four Dervishes

The Tale of the Four Dervishes

The Tale of the Four Dervishes (*Ghasseh-e Chahar Dervish*, Persian قصه چهار درویش) is a collection of allegorical stories by Amir Khusro written in Persian in the late 13th century.

Legend has it that Amir Khusro's master and Sufi saint Nizamuddin Auliya had fallen ill. To cheer him up, Amir Khusro started telling him a series of stories in Hazar-o yek shab (Arabian Nights) style. By the end of the stories, Nizamuddin Auliya had recovered, and prayed that anyone who listened to these stories would also be cured.

Style

The book is in some ways similar to the Thousand and one nights in its method of dovetailing unfinished stories within each other. The central character is a king, Azad Bakht, who falls into depression after thinking about his own mortality, and so sets out from his palace seeking wise men. He comes upon four dervishes in a cemetery, and listens in to their fantastical stories.

Translations

These stories were originally written in Persian by Amir Khusro as "Ghasseh-e Chahar Darvesh" (The Tale of the Four Dervishes). It was initially translated by an unknown author into Urdu but the language was a highly literate one and was not understood by general public to enjoy. In 1801, College of Fort William in Calcutta started a project translating Indian literature. Mr. John Borthwick Gilchrist, a famous scholar of literature, asked Mir Amman, an employee of the college, to translate it into the Urdu language. Mir Amman translated it from Persian into everyday Urdu, under the title *Bagh o Bahar* (The Garden and the Spring Season). Later, in 1857, Duncan Forbes retranslated it into English. The translation of Mir Amman is still enjoyed as a classical work of literature for the common daily language of its time.

See also

- One Thousand and One Nights
- Hamzanama

External links

- Bagh O Bahar, or Tales of the Four Dervishes Online [1]
- Bagh O Bahar for download [2]
- Ancient love stories [3]

Yusuf and Zulaikha

Yusuf and Zulaikha

Yusuf and Zulaikha is the Quranic verse of Yusuf (Joseph) and Zulaikha (the person known in the Bible as Potiphar's wife and whose name is not given there). It has been told and retold countless times in many languages spoken by Muslims, especially Persian. Its most famous version was written in Persian by Jami (1414-1492), in his *Haft Awrang* ("Seven Thrones").

Other writers to have retold the story include: Mahmud Gami (Kashmiri). It is a standard tale used in Punjabi Qisse.

Also there exists a long poem on the subject, titled as Yusuf and Zalikha, which used to be attributed to Ferdowsi, the great Persian poet of the tenth and eleventh century, however, the scholars have rejected this book based on its low quality and the time line of Ferdowsi's life.

'Yusuf and Zalikha: The Biblical Legend of Joseph and Potiphar's Wife in the Persian Version Ascribed to Abul-Mansur Qasim, Called Firdausi, ca. 932-1021 A.D.,' Edited by Hermann Ethé, Philo Press, Amsterdam, 1970

External links

- English translation of Jami's Joseph and Zuleika (edited by Charles Horne, 1917) [1] PDF (138 KiB)
- *Women Writers, Islam, and the Ghost of Zulaikha* [2], by Elif Shafak
- *The story of Yusuf and Zulaikha in the Quran* [3]
- *The story of Yusuf and Zilayxa translated from a Uyghur (North West China) text* [4]
- The story of Yusuf and Zulaikha in the Quran [5] The same article is also available at [6], [3]

Momal Rano

Momal Rano

Momal Rano (Sindhi مومل راڻو)is one of the historical tales and is the rich history of the soil of Pakistan. It is one of the four popular tragic romances of South Asian literature. The other three are Heer Ranjha, Sassi Punnun and Sohni Mahiwal.

Momal was a gorgeous princess and living at Ghotki in a glamorous palace named **Kak Mahal** in Pakistan. Her people created a magical erection over 22 of 55 which are there in Kak Mahal. A magnetic field was spread over the ground which was giving a transitory look like hasty waves of big river. As well a precarious jungle was fashioned, this occupied with animals including lions, tigers, etc. Princess Momal would marry with the man who would come to Kak Mahal and cross that magnetic fields with bravery. Many of the princes who have heard about the beauty of Momal have tried to get married to her, but failed to cross the Kak Mahal's magnetic field.

Rano was one of those who heard about the beauty of princess Momal and was one of the contenders who tried to go to Kak Mahal to win the fair lady's heart. Rano was a wise man and understood the magical strategy of Kak Mahal and reached to Momal and got married with her.

See also

- LiLa Chanesar
- Umar Marvi
- Noori Jam Tamachi
- Sindhi literature
- Shah Abdul Latif Bhittai
- Pakistani Folklore

External links

- Mumal and Rano [1] by Elsa Qazi

Umar Marvi

Umar Marvi

Umar Marvi (Sindhi: عمر ماروي) is a Sindh love story that appears in *Shah Jo Risalo*. It is a love story set in Sindh, Pakistan. It has become part of the cultural identity of Pakistan, as have stories like *Sassi Punnun*, *Heer Ranjha*, and *Sohni Mahiwal*.

Synopsis

Marvi (Sindhi: ماروي) was a Sindhi heroine famous for her chastity, patriotism, and simplicity. Phog (Sindhi: □و□), an orphan boy, lived with Marvi's family. As children, Marvi and Phog played together. Attracted by Marvi's beauty, he wanted to marry her, but Marvi had always treated him like a brother. She told him not to expect anything beyond that. Rebuffed, Phog sulked and withdrew. Marvi found her ideal in Khet, a cousin who lived in a neighbouring village. He was handsome and brave, and he was deeply in love with Marvi. She lived in a village called Malir in Tharparkar desert. She was a beautiful village girl and was engaged to her cousin Khet (Sindhi: کيت). One day while she was filling water in her pots from a well (now called "Marvi's Well" (Sindhi: ماروي جو کو□) *Marvi jo khooh*) to provide water for her goats, was seen by Prince Umar Soomro (Sindhi: عمر سومرو). Umar (Sindhi: عمر) was immediately dazzled by her beauty. Umar proposed to marry her and tried to win her over with jewels and gifts, but Marvi refused, as she was deeply devoted to her cousin. Angered by her refusals, Umar abducted her and imprisoned her his palace in Umerkot for a whole year, but she remained faithful and longed for her native terrain. Finally, Umar was deeply touched by her dedication and piety and set Marvi free.

Umar knowing about Marvi

In those days Sindh was ruled by Umar Soomro, whose capital was Umarkot, now in Pakistan. He was known for his justice. He had only one weakness: he loved beautiful women. His palace was full of beautiful damsels from all parts of Sindh. Phog left Malir and went to Umarkot to seek his fortune. He managed to secure employment under Umar. He soon won Umar's confidence and was put to work managing matters relating to women. One day he told Umar about the most beautiful woman in Sindh. Curious, the Umar asked, "Who is she?" Phog replied, "Her name is Marvi."

Adaptations

Umar Marvi was recreated in Pakistan in the form of a television series recreating the story of Marvi in a more modern setting, where Marvi is depicted as a Sindhi village girl who is educated and wants to go to the city for further education. Marvi's best friend, with whom she dorms in the city, has a brother named Umar who falls in love with her and proposes to her. Upon Marvi's refusal to marry him he consults his friend, a rich land owner in Marvi's village. The two devise a plan to abduct Marvi and keep her at Umar Sommro's mansion. Marvi somehow manages to escape from Umar Summro's, but upon her return, the villagers demand where she has been and question her chastity. Marvi's friend, who is aware of her brother's acts, consults a journalist and a lawyer to have her brother arrested for kidnapping. During the trial, Marvi has to face all kinds of questions about her piety and chastity, but finally Umar stands up in the courtroom and admits he is guilty and that Marvi is indeed a woman of great character.

See also

- Sindhi literature
- Heer Ranjha
- Momal Rano
- Sassi Punnun
- LiLa Chanesar
- Sohni Mahiwal
- Noori Jam Tamachi
- Shah Jo Risalo

LiLa Chanesar

LiLa Chanesar

LiLa Chanesar(Sindhi: لیلا چنیسر), is a Sindhi folk story found in Shah Jo Risalo, written by Bhittai. Raja Chanesar was a well known ruler of the Soomro dynasty, who ruled Dewal (Sindh). He had a beautiful queen Lila, who was very fond of Diamonds and Jewellery.

Contemporary to him was Rana Khanghar, who ruled Lakhpat in Kutchh. He had an only daughter Kaunru, who was very beautiful and engaged to her cousin Utmadi. Being the only daughter of Rana Khanghar and Mirkhi, too much love had spoiled her. She was proud of her beauty and was always worried about her looks. One day her friend Jamni who was the sister of Utmadi teased Kaunru about her attitude, saying she was behaving as if she would be the queen of Chanesar. Kaunru was hurt and told her mother that either she would have to marry Chanesar, or she would commit suicide. Her parents were alarmed, but they were aware that Chanaesar was married and loved his queen Lila very much.

After consulting her husband, Mirkhi and Kaunru disguised themselves as traders and left for Dewal. There they managed to consult Jakhiro the king's minister and asked him to help them. He promised he would persuade Chanesar to marry Kaunru.

When Jakhiro spoke to Chanesar about Kaunru, the king lost his temper and told him that he should not talk like that in future. In Lila's presence he could not even think about any other woman. Jakhiro offered his apologies to Mirkhi and Kaunru and told them that there was no hope, and that it was therefore useless for them to try.

Kaunru and her mother put on ordinary dresses to disguise themselves and went to Lila's palace. There they asked Lila to employ them in her service, as they had abandoned their country because of poverty. Lila felt sorry for them and employed them as personal servants. Kaunru was asked to arrange Chanesar's bed every day. Time passed without any hope of success.

One day as Kaunru was preparing the bed for Chanesar, tears dropped from her eyes. Lila, who had entered the room unnoticed, saw Kaunru's tears. She asked the reason for the tears. Kaunru told her that at one time she had also been a princess and had lived a luxurious life like her. She told her that instead of using lanterns and lamps she used to light her palace with 'Naulakha Har' (a necklace worth 900,000 rupees).

At first, Lila was hesitant to believe her but she soon became anxious to see that necklace. When Kaunru showed her, Lila asked her for what price she was prepared to part with it. Kanuru told Lila that she would give her necklace free to her but on one condition. Lila became impatient and asked for the condition. Kaunru told her that the necklace would be hers if she would just let her spend one night with Chanesar.

When Lila spoke to Chanesar he did not approve of her idea. One day, Chanesar came home after a party and was heavily drunk. Lila considered it her best opportunity and she allowed Kaunru into her bedroom. In the morning when Chanesar woke up, he was shocked to see Kaunru instead of Lila sharing his bed. He was very angry and was about to leave the room, when Mirkhi (Kaunru's mother) told him that Lila had sold him to Kaunru in return for the 'Naulakha Har'. Chanesar considered it an insult and humilitation to be exchanged for a mere necklace.

As his revenge, he deserted Lila and married Kaunru who had given so much sacrifice for him. Lila tried to apologize, cried and begged but Chanesar refused to listen to her, saying that she had preferred jewellery to him and that he did not Love her any more. Lila after giving up all hope left his house and went to her parents. There she spent her days in misery, solitude and repentance. Jakhiro who was the minister of Chanesar was engaged to one of the girls from Lila's family. But they refused to give her hand to him after the fate of Lila. The minister approached Lila who intervened but asked him to bring Chanesar on his wedding, to which he happily agreed. On the occasion of Jakhiro's wedding Chanesar came along with the bridegroom party. Lila with other girls welcomed the party with dancing and singing but her face was Veiled. Chanesar was pleased at their performance and he was especially fascinated at the dancing and the voice of the one whose face was veiled. Chanesar begged the girl to unveil her face as he could not tolerate the situation any more. As soon as Lila opened her veil Chanesar fell down on the floor and died. When Lila saw this she also died.

See also

- Heer Ranjha
- Momal Rano
- Sassi Punnun
- Sohni Mahiwal
- Noori Jam Tamachi
- Sindhi literature
- Shah Jo Risalo

External links

- [1](Leela, Elsa Qazi).

Hani and Sheh Mureed

Hani and Sheh Mureed

Hani and Sheh Mureed or **Murid** (Balochi **Hanee-o-Shay Mureed** or ***Hero Šey Murīd***) is a beloved epic ballad of Balochi folklore.This tale is to Balochistan what Romeo and Juliet is to English-speaking lands.The story mirrors the life of the Baloch heroes and their emotions and philosophical ideas (God, evil, predestination).The hero of the story, Sheh Mureed (or Shaih Moreed) and the heroine Hani are symbols of pure and tragic love. The story dates back to the 15th century, which is considered to be the heroic age of Balochistan and the classical period of Balochi literature.

Characters

Sheh Murid

Sheh Murid was the son of Sheh Mubarak, the chief of the Kahiri tribe. At that time when a man was known for his arts, Murid was famous as having mastered the art of swordmanship, horsemanship, and archery. For his skills and braveness he was ranked the highest in the army of Mir Chakar Khan Rind, the chief of the Kahiri army. Murid's bow made of steel was so heavy that he was known as the "Lord of the Iron Bow", because none but he alone could draw and shoot arrows from it.

Hani

Hani was the daughter of the Rind noble Mir Mandaw; it is clear from epic poems she is fether mentioned as Dinar, some say she was Murid's cousin. Hani was a paragon of loyalty and devotion. Everyone knew her for her good character and chastity. Hani was engaged to Sheh Murid and had been a childhood friend of Murid.

Story

The legend is that one day when Mir Chakar and Sheh Murid were returning from a day of hunting, they stopped at the town where their fiancées lived. Since a Muslim Balochistani Baloch woman traditionally never appears before her betrothed before the wedding, Mir Chakar and Sheh Murid decide to visit each others' fiancées. Sheh Murid went to Mir Chakar's fiancée, who brought him clean water in a silver bowl. Murid, dying of thirst, drank the entire bowl in a single gulp and became sick. However, when Mir Chakar went to Hani, Sheh Murid's fiancée, she brought him clean water in a silver bowl in which she has placed dwarf palm leaf, properly washed. The chief was surprised by the pieces of straw, but he drank the water with care in order to avoid swallowing the straw. When he departed he found Murid vomiting and sick. Murid told him that the water had made him ill because he drank a lot of water on an empty stomach. Now Mir Chakar realized that Hani had acted wisely by putting pieces of straw ino the water.

Some time later, Mir Chakar organized a gathering where poets put forward poetry of heroes etc. At the height of the revelry Mir Chakar asked the nobles to make vows on which they must pledge their lives. Every chief at the gathering made a vow. Mir Jado swore that he would chop off the head of anyone who touched his beard at the assembly of nobles. Then Bibarg vowed that he would kill anyone who kills Hadeh. He was followed by Mir Haibitan who vowed that if anybody's camel joined his camel-herd he would never give it back. At last came the turn of Sheh Murid, who, madly in love with Hani, pledged that if anyone asked for anything in his possession on his wedding day, he would give it. Later on, Mir Chakar vowed that he would never tell a lie for the rest of his life. He was true to his word: He never in his lifetime after that was found to have lied. Mir Chakar tested Mir Jado's word by asking his young son to touch his father's beard during an assembly of nobles. The young boy innocently did as he was told, Mir Jado turned his face and moved the boy hoping no one noticed. However Mir Chakar encouraged the boy to repeat the action. the boy grabbed his father's beard once more. The entire assembly became silent and looked towards Mir Jado. Will he be true to his word? Full of wrath, Jado unsheathes his sword and smites the head of his innocent son in the presence of all the Rind nobles. Mir Chakar also tested Bibarg and Haibitan, finding them true to their word. Now it was time to test Sheh Murid. Murid hosted a festive gathering on his wedding and invited renowned poets to entertain the audience. And at the close of the festivities, Sheh Murid, was ready to depart with his possessions. Mir Chakar asked for Hani. Sheh Murid was shocked; he thought that he would have asked for his bow which was a unique bow and he was a very good marksmen with a strong bow. He was known as The Lord Of The Iron Bow. With a heavy heart and much sadness he told Mir Chakar to take Hani. The unexpected demand distressed him greatly, and Murid realized that he had lost Hani. If he did not keep his vow he would be mocked and future generations would have contempt for his name. Soon after the annulment of Murid's engagement with Hani, she was soon married to Mir Chakar. But Murid was so shaken by this turn of events that he abandoned his former life and passed the days and nights in worship of Allah. He also composed poems eulogizing Hani's beauty and openly expressing his passionate love for her. The scandalous news of Murid's love for Mir Chakar's wife became the talk of every household in Balochistan. His father Sheh Mubarak tried to advise him, he composed a poem in Baluchi of the advice that his father gave him and the response to the advice. The poem in Baluchi is as follows:

Baluchi	English
mani shehey mubarak gwashee	My Shai mubarak says,
bellow mureed gumraheeya,	Oh Mureed leave your aloofness,
gumraheeya be raheya	Aloofness without purpose direction(purpose),
pa chaakare mahay janna.	For chakars beautiful wife,
pa dosti dosta e nahay	In the assemblies you are not amongst your friends,
jaan ahay pashentagay,	You are like a walking corpse,
hani sha kour-ka geptagay	Hani's love has blinded you,
zay chond-dilla cho beetagay.	How will you carry on in this way,
man jawab tarentaga,	I replied,
peeray pitto cho gwashtaga,	I advised my elderly father,
wati meeray pito cho gwashtaga,	I advised my respected father,
shai abaee shai kabaee,	Oh most honoured father,
agay takay bibiten hat-tali	Oh most esteemed,
pahoukana hancho dost mani,	If you were in my place likewise,
shalwaray bonday darr kutain	You would have left all your friends,
janay darre pakko kutain,	And stopped going to assemblies and noble gatherings,
lenchan wati jattay,	You would have lost your mind,
hanga mano gah-bo-waton gah-be-waton	And not be aware of how you dressed,
	You would have clapped your hands,
	On your lap and be,
	In your own world,
	At least i am sometimes with it
	And sometimes not with it.

Departure and return

Sheh Murid then decided to leave the country and visit unknown lands across the seas. He followed a group of mendicants going to perform their pilgrimage at the holy cities of Mecca and Medina in Arabia. As tradition has it, Sheh Murid remained in Arabia for 30 a long time during which time he truly became a mendicant and lived the life of an ascetic.

After spending years away, he returned to Sibi in shabby clothes with his hair hanging down to his waist. In the company of a band of beggars he passed himself off as an anonymous mendicant begging for alms at the palace of Mir Chakar Khan Rind. The maidservant gave bowls filled with grain to each mendicant, but when she presented this food to Murid, she saw that Murid's eyes were fixed upon Hani. Hani recognised him at once but held herself back as to not arise suspicions, but Chakar saw a sparkle in her eyes.

Recognition of Sheh Murid

As a favorite pastime of the Chakarian age, the Rind nobles gathered for an archery competition. During the contest, the nobles noticed the curiosity and interest of Murid, the leader of beggars. At first the Rind nobles treated him with a certain amount of disrespect on account of his shabby appearance, laughing at him and asking how a mendicant clad in tattered clothes could bend a bow and hit a target. They gave him a bow and arrow. He bent the bow but it could not bear the power of his arms and broke into pieces. They gave him another one, which he also broke. After he broke the third bow the Rind nobles grow a bit suspicious that he might be Sheh Murid. They sent someone to fetch Murid Khan's bow, which was made out of steel and was called *jug* (yoke) because of its form and weight. The epic tells us that this famous weapon had been tossed in a pen for sheep and goats after the "master of the iron bow" had departed and it had no owner to care for it. Because of its weight and toughness, it was useless in the hands of anyone else. When it was turned over to him, Sheh Murid caressed and kissed it, gently touching the strings as if they belonged to a sacred instrument; he scrutinized every inch. Then, as a master archer, he rolled up his beggar's mantle, bent the bow with great skill, and shot three arrows from it, passing one through the hole left by the previous one. The Rind's suspicion that this beggar was in fact Sheh Murid was confirmed after the trial of the bow. The Rind nobles stopped Murid and a servant was sent to ask Hani for Murid's distinguishing signs and marks, which she would know because they had played together as children. Hani told of a sign on the upper left thigh, which her bracelet had made, and another one behind the eyebrow. When the Rinds checked the signs, they at last recognized Sheh Murid.

Union and departure to unknown world

Although Mir Chakar married Hani, however he was unable to consummate the marriage, Whenever he approached Hani, he would freeze as if paralyzed. For years he carried on this way and realised that Hani can never truly be his. When he found out that Sheh Murid had returned, he Told Hani that Sheh Murid was a great man and deserved her, so he divorced her and told her she was free to go to Sheh Murid

Hani, who had not forgotten her first and only love, decided to go to him, she told him that Mir Chakar had realised his mistake and has now freed her so that they (i.e. Sheh Murid& Hani) could be together. But Sheh Murid told her that he had now reached a different level and cannot step down from that level to take her she was a means by which he had reached closer to Allah. He took leave of her.. On the following day Murid visited his father's camel herd, chose a white she-camel, mounted her, and disappeared from mortal eyes. He has become the immortal saint of the Baloch, and the common belief among the Baloch is that: *ta jahan ast, Sheh Murid ast* (Until the living world, Sheh Murid remains immortal.)

See also

- Mir Chakar Khan Rind
- Rind

References

- "Lord of the Iron Bow": The Return Pattern Motif in the Fifteenth-century Baloch Epic Hero Sey Murid [1] (PDF)
- Popular Poetry of the Baloches [2]

Article Sources and Contributors

Heer Ranjha *Source*: http://en.wikipedia.org/?oldid=379951466 *Contributors*: Fayenatic london

Mirza Sahiba *Source*: http://en.wikipedia.org/?oldid=390088606 *Contributors*: 1 anonymous edits

Sohni Mahiwal *Source*: http://en.wikipedia.org/?oldid=389613672 *Contributors*:

Punjabi Kisse *Source*: http://en.wikipedia.org/?oldid=387290751 *Contributors*: Rjwilmsi

Sucha Singh Soorma *Source*: http://en.wikipedia.org/?oldid=379768456 *Contributors*: Jodi.a.schneider

Sanwal Sajal *Source*: http://en.wikipedia.org/?oldid=352349562 *Contributors*: John of Reading

Punjabi folklore *Source*: http://en.wikipedia.org/?oldid=389287514 *Contributors*: Tmorton166

Sassi Punnun *Source*: http://en.wikipedia.org/?oldid=389613655 *Contributors*:

Dhaj, Ror Kumar *Source*: http://en.wikipedia.org/?oldid=389613691 *Contributors*:

Shahrukh Husain *Source*: http://en.wikipedia.org/?oldid=388125473 *Contributors*: Xezbeth

Jinn *Source*: http://en.wikipedia.org/?oldid=390682561 *Contributors*: 1 anonymous edits

One Thousand and One Nights *Source*: http://en.wikipedia.org/?oldid=390604315 *Contributors*: Soundofmusicals

Hamzanama *Source*: http://en.wikipedia.org/?oldid=385962674 *Contributors*:

Lake Saiful Muluk *Source*: http://en.wikipedia.org/?oldid=388071267 *Contributors*: Spasage

Churel *Source*: http://en.wikipedia.org/?oldid=332062047 *Contributors*:

Pakistani folklore *Source*: http://en.wikipedia.org/?oldid=389867720 *Contributors*: AtticusX

Ayyār *Source*: http://en.wikipedia.org/?oldid=382224231 *Contributors*: 1 anonymous edits

Adam Khan and Durkhanai *Source*: http://en.wikipedia.org/?oldid=234024171 *Contributors*: Cuchullain

Yusuf Khan and Sherbano *Source*: http://en.wikipedia.org/?oldid=382903064 *Contributors*:

Prince Saiful Malook and Badri Jamala *Source*: http://en.wikipedia.org/?oldid=390600994 *Contributors*: Sarabseth

Noori Jam Tamachi *Source*: http://en.wikipedia.org/?oldid=378753725 *Contributors*: Xeno

The Tale of the Four Dervishes *Source*: http://en.wikipedia.org/?oldid=370594036 *Contributors*: 1 anonymous edits

Yusuf and Zulaikha *Source*: http://en.wikipedia.org/?oldid=365621994 *Contributors*: Good Olfactory

Momal Rano *Source*: http://en.wikipedia.org/?oldid=386789418 *Contributors*: Xeno

Umar Marvi *Source*: http://en.wikipedia.org/?oldid=388616941 *Contributors*: AtticusX

LiLa Chanesar *Source*: http://en.wikipedia.org/?oldid=364569800 *Contributors*: 1 anonymous edits

Hani and Sheh Mureed *Source*: http://en.wikipedia.org/?oldid=380745842 *Contributors*: 1 anonymous edits

Image Sources, Licenses and Contributors

File:Tilla Jogian.jpg *Source*: http://en.wikipedia.org/w/index.php?title=File:Tilla_Jogian.jpg *License*: unknown *Contributors*: -

File:Descending into cave.jpg *Source*: http://en.wikipedia.org/w/index.php?title=File:Descending_into_cave.jpg *License*: GNU Free Documentation License *Contributors*: Original uploader was Michaelmcandrew at en.wikipedia

File:1001-nights.jpg *Source*: http://en.wikipedia.org/w/index.php?title=File:1001-nights.jpg *License*: Public Domain *Contributors*: Cookie, Fito hg, Judithcomm, Juiced lemon, Svencb, 3 anonymous edits

File:Sultan Pardons Scheherazade.jpg *Source*: http://en.wikipedia.org/w/index.php?title=File:Sultan_Pardons_Scheherazade.jpg *License*: Public Domain *Contributors*: Cookie, Fito hg, Judithcomm, Mutter Erde, 2 anonymous edits

File:Kelileh va Demneh.jpg *Source*: http://en.wikipedia.org/w/index.php?title=File:Kelileh_va_Demneh.jpg *License*: unknown *Contributors*: User Zereshk on en.wikipedia

File:1001 nights Russian poster - flickr - 1.JPG *Source*: http://en.wikipedia.org/w/index.php?title=File:1001_nights_Russian_poster_-_flickr_-_1.JPG *License*: unknown *Contributors*: Alex Bakharev, Eintragung ins Nichts, HHHH, Man vyi, Shtanga, 1 anonymous edits

File:Arabian nights manuscript.jpg *Source*: http://en.wikipedia.org/w/index.php?title=File:Arabian_nights_manuscript.jpg *License*: Public Domain *Contributors*: Aziz1005, K.C. Tang, Philip Stevens, Santosga, Solbris, WolfgangRieger

Image:Indischer Maler um 1580 001.jpg *Source*: http://en.wikipedia.org/w/index.php?title=File:Indischer_Maler_um_1580_001.jpg *License*: Public Domain *Contributors*: Abhishekjoshi, AndreasPraefcke, Calame, Johnbod, Killiondude, Roland zh, Tiptoety, Wst, 3 anonymous edits

Image:Sughrat.jpg *Source*: http://en.wikipedia.org/w/index.php?title=File:Sughrat.jpg *License*: Public Domain *Contributors*: Ilse@, Pieter Kuiper, Shizhao, Tomisti, Urban, 1 anonymous edits

File:One Thousand and One Nights19.jpg *Source*: http://en.wikipedia.org/w/index.php?title=File:One_Thousand_and_One_Nights19.jpg *License*: Public Domain *Contributors*: Sani ol-Molk

File:The battle of Mazandaran.jpg *Source*: http://en.wikipedia.org/w/index.php?title=File:The_battle_of_Mazandaran.jpg *License*: unknown *Contributors*: -

file:Saif ul muluk.jpg *Source*: http://en.wikipedia.org/w/index.php?title=File:Saif_ul_muluk.jpg *License*: unknown *Contributors*: -

Image:Saiful muluk during June.JPG *Source*: http://en.wikipedia.org/w/index.php?title=File:Saiful_muluk_during_June.JPG *License*: unknown *Contributors*: -

Image:BridgeatSaifalMalook.JPG *Source*: http://en.wikipedia.org/w/index.php?title=File:BridgeatSaifalMalook.JPG *License*: unknown *Contributors*: -

Image:Nasreddin.jpg *Source*: http://en.wikipedia.org/w/index.php?title=File:Nasreddin.jpg *License*: GNU Free Documentation License *Contributors*: DrKiernan, Hunadam, Te5, Wst

CPSIA information can be obtained at www.ICGtesting.com
Printed in the USA
LVOW111935151112
307509LV00007B/123/P

9 781244 302303